THE NEW LAWYER'S WIT AND WISDOM

THE NEW LAWYER'S WIT AND WISDOM

Quotations on the Legal Profession, In Brief

Edited by Bruce Nash, Allan Zullo
Compiled by Kathryn Zullo

THIRD INDIAN REPRINT, 2011

Universal
Law Publishing Co. Pvt. Ltd.
NEW DELHI - INDIA

First Indian Reprint 2001
Second Indian Reprint 2007
Third Indian Reprint 2011

ISBN: 978-81-7534-632-1

Published by
UNIVERSAL LAW PUBLISHING CO. PVT. LTD.
C-FF-1A, Dilkhush Industrial Estate (Near Azadpur Metro Station)
G.T. Karnal Road, Delhi-110 033
Tel.: 011- 42381334, 27215334, 27438103, Fax : 011-27458529
E-mail *(For sales inquiries)* : sales@unilawbooks.com
Website : www.unilawbooks.com

Under special arrangement with
RUNNING PRESS BOOK PUBLISHERS, U.S.A.

Library of Congress Cataloging-in-Publication number 2001087059

Licensed for sale in Indian sub-continent

Cover design by Kori Klyman
Cover photograph: © Chris Collins/Corbis/Stockmarket
Interior design by Paul Kepple and Serrin Bodmer
Interior illustrations by Tim Lewis
Edited by Melissa Wagner
Typography: Copperplate and Goudy

Printed in India at Glorious Printers, New Delhi

DEDICATION

To Marty Groothuis, a negotiator extraordinaire, who could teach Donald Trump a thing or two about the art of the deal.

—BRUCE NASH

To Larry Murphy, who practices law the only way he knows how—with honesty and integrity.

—ALLAN ZULLO

To my son-in-law Danny Manausa, who is now a member of the bar, rather than just a patron of one.

—KATHRYN ZULLO

CONTENTS

Acknowledgements 9
Introduction 10

THE PEOPLE 13

The Law 15
Lawyers 38
Clients 65
Law Firms 77
Judges 82
Juries 98
Witnesses 109
The Supreme Court 113

CODES OF CONDUCT 118

Ethics 121
Government 130
Law School 137
Obeying the Law 143
Justice 153
Injustice 173

THE WHEELS OF JUSTICE 180

Litigation 183
The Trial 192
The Verdict 200

CLOSING ARGUMENTS 206

The Profession 209
Legal Fees 222
Courtroom Performance 229
The System 238
On Reform 256
Advice to Lawyers 265

Index of Names 274

ACKNOWLEDGEMENTS

The authors wish to thank the American Bar Association for its cooperation in allowing us to adapt many of the anecdotes in this book from two of its publications.

Several anecdotes were first reported in the monthly "War Stories" feature in the *ABA Journal*, which graciously granted us permission to edit and reprint them.

Other anecdotes were adapted from an annual feature called "Legal Lunacies" by Barbara Kate Repa, which appeared between 1985 and 1993 in *Student Lawyer* magazine, also published by the American Bar Association. *Student Lawyer* granted us permission to edit and reprint these items, for which we are grateful.

Finally, the authors wish to thank *Reader's Digest* for allowing us to reprint five anecdotes that had originally appeared in earlier issues.

INTRODUCTION

No group is exalted or vilified more than lawyers. In Shakespeare's Henry VI, Part II, Act IV, Dick the butcher fantasizes: "The first thing we do, let's kill all the lawyers"—probably the world's favorite quote regarding the profession. But before Dick's sympathizers judge too quickly, they should at least weigh the testimony of well-known defense attorney Ellis Rubin: "Being a lawyer is about serving justice. That's not only our greatest calling, it's our only calling."

The legal profession triggers diverse opinions and feelings because lawyers deal with extremes of the human condition, usually interacting with people in times of great need and stress. As famed jurist Oliver Wendell Holmes Jr. once said, "In what other [profession]

DOES ONE PLUNGE SO DEEP IN THE STREAM OF LIFE, SO SHARE ITS PASSIONS, ITS BATTLES, ITS DESPAIR, ITS TRIUMPHS, BOTH AS WITNESS AND ACTOR?"

ALTHOUGH THE LAW HAS CHANGED OVER THE CENTURIES, THE RELATIONSHIP BETWEEN ATTORNEYS AND CLIENTS HAS REMAINED PRETTY MUCH THE SAME—IT'S STILL A LOVE-HATE AFFAIR. NO WONDER PEOPLE FROM ALL WALKS OF LIFE HAVE NEVER BEEN AT A LOSS FOR WORDS WHEN REVEALING THEIR TRUE FEELINGS ABOUT LAWYERS. IN THIS BOOK, THE QUOTATIONS RANGE FROM INSIGHTFUL AND PITHY QUOTES FROM FAMOUS JUDGES AND PHILOSOPHERS TO LIGHT-HEARTED QUIPS FROM FICTIONAL CHARACTERS AND SATIRISTS. AND SOMETIMES TRUTH IS STRANGER THAN FICTION, AS THE LEAVENING OF HUMOROUS TRUE-LIFE ANECDOTES ABOUT LIFE IN THE LEGAL WORLD PROVES.

WORDS HAVE BEEN—AND ALWAYS WILL BE—THE BASIC TOOLS OF THE LAWYER. SAID NOTED LEGAL SCHOLAR CHARLES ALAN WRIGHT, "WHETHER WE ARE TRYING A CASE, WRITING A BRIEF, DRAFTING A CONTRACT, OR NEGOTIATING WITH AN ADVERSARY, WORDS ARE THE ONLY THINGS WE HAVE TO WORK WITH."

THE PEOPLE

THE LAW

Common sense often makes a good law.

WILLIAM O. DOUGLAS,
SUPREME COURT JUSTICE

If you like laws and sausages, you should never watch either one being made.

OTTO VON BISMARCK,
19TH-CENTURY PRUSSIAN PRINCE

The citizen is the law. In this country we haven't got around to understanding that. We think of the law as an enemy.

RAYMOND CHANDLER,
AMERICAN MYSTERY AND SUSPENSE NOVELIST

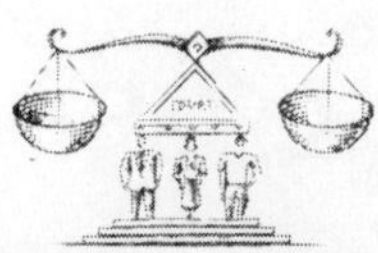

It is a besetting vice of democracies to substitute public opinion for law. This is the usual form in which masses of men exhibit their tyranny.

JAMES FENIMORE COOPER,
AMERICAN NOVELIST

The law is not a machine and the judges not machine-tenders. There never was and there never will be a body of fixed and predetermined rules alike for all.

JEROME N. FRANK,
AMERICAN JUDGE

From Watergate we learned what generations before us have known—our Constitution works. And during Watergate years it was interpreted again so as to reaffirm that no one—absolutely no one—is above the law.

LEON JAWORSKI,
SPECIAL PROSECUTOR FOR WATERGATE TRIALS

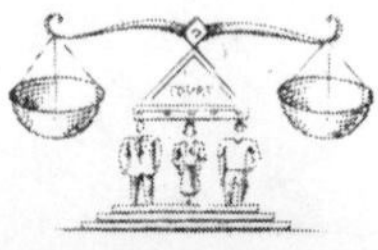

Without the law, there can be no justice.
And without justice, there can be no freedom.

SAM WATERSTON AS JACK MCCOY,
DISTRICT ATTORNEY IN THE TELEVISION SHOW LAW AND ORDER

No law or ordinance is mightier than understanding.

PLATO,
1ST-CENTURY GREEK PHILOSOPHER

To be effective, a law must have the support of the majority of people it impacts. To get that support, a law must be enforceable, fairly applied, understood, and consistent with society's values.

THOMAS A. WARTOWSKI,
AMERICAN LAWYER

I decided law was the exact opposite of sex; even when it was good it was lousy.

MORTIMER ZUCKERMAN,
AMERICAN JOURNALIST

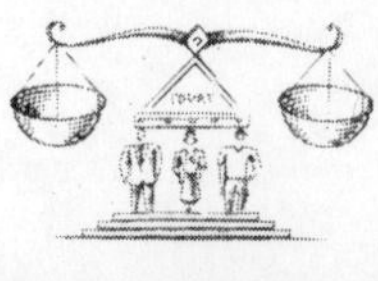

The law is like the killy-loo bird, a creature that insisted on flying backward because it didn't care where it was going but was mightily interested where it had been.

FRED RODELL,
LAW PROFESSOR, YALE UNIVERSITY

All laws are an attempt to domesticate the natural ferocity of the species.

JOHN W. GARDNER,
U.S. SECRETARY OF HEALTH, EDUCATION, AND WELFARE

Law is born from despair of human nature.

JOSE ORTEGA Y GASSET,
19TH-CENTURY SPANISH PHILOSOPHER

The laws sometimes sleep, but never die.

ANONYMOUS

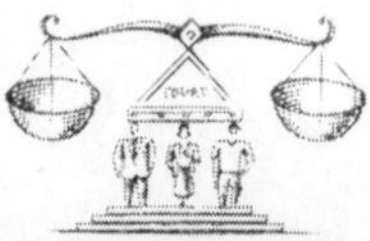

The law, in its majestic equality, forbids all men to sleep under bridges, to beg in the streets, and to steal bread—the rich as well as the poor.

ANATOLE FRANCE,
FRENCH WRITER

The wording of laws should mean the same thing to all men.

CHARLES LOUIS DE MONTESQUIEU,
17TH-CENTURY FRENCH LAWYER AND POLITICAL PHILOSOPHER

Laws are felt only when the individual comes into conflict with them.

SUZANNE LA FOLLETTE,
AMERICAN POLITICIAN AND FEMINIST

Where-ever Law ends, Tyranny begins.

JOHN LOCKE,
17TH-CENTURY ENGLISH PHILOSOPHER

Law is a pledge that the citizens of a state will do justice to one another.

LYCOPHRON,
3RD-CENTURY B.C. GREEK POET AND SCHOLAR

The law: It has honored us; may we honor it.

DANIEL WEBSTER,
18TH-CENTURY AMERICAN STATESMAN, ORATOR, AND LAWYER

If we desire respect for the law we must first make the law respectable.

LOUIS D. BRANDEIS,
SUPREME COURT JUSTICE

Good laws lead to the making of better ones; bad ones bring about worse.

JEAN JACQUES ROUSSEAU,
18TH-CENTURY FRENCH PHILOSOPHER AND WRITER

Riches without law are more dangerous than is poverty without law.

HENRY WARD BEECHER,
19TH-CENTURY AMERICAN CLERGYMAN

I say that you cannot administer a wicked law impartially. You can only destroy. You can only punish. I warn you that a wicked law, like cholera, destroys everyone it touches—its upholders as well as its defiers.

SPENCER TRACY AS HENRY DRUMMOND
IN THE FILM INHERIT THE WIND

Nothing is more destructive of respect for the government and the law of the land than passing laws which cannot be enforced.

ALBERT EINSTEIN,
GERMAN-BORN AMERICAN PHYSICIST

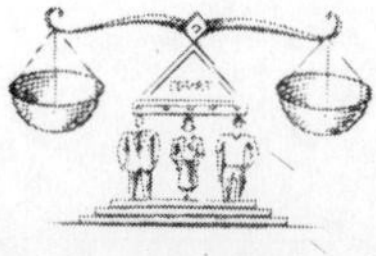

It may be true that the law cannot make
a man love me, but it can keep him from
lynching me, and I think that's pretty important.

**DR. MARTIN LUTHER KING, JR.,
AMERICAN CLERGYMAN
AND CIVIL RIGHTS LEADER**

Whereas the law is passionless, passion must
never sway the heart of man.

**ARISTOTLE,
4TH-CENTURY B.C. GREEK PHILOSOPHER**

Law is a Bottomless-Pit, it is a Cormorant,
a Harpy, that devours every thing.

**JOHN ARBUTHNOT,
17TH-CENTURY SCOTTISH PHYSICIAN AND WRITER**

Law: an ordinance of reason for the common good,
made by him who has care of the community.

**ST. THOMAS AQUINAS,
13TH-CENTURY ITALIAN THEOLOGIAN**

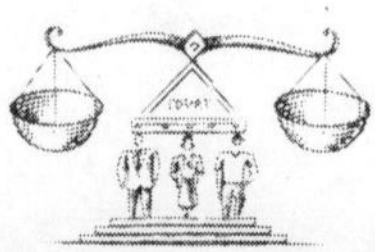

The good of the people is the supreme law.

CICERO,
2ND-CENTURY B.C. ROMAN STATESMAN,
ORATOR, AND WRITER

Law is a formless mass of isolated decisions.

MORRIS COHEN,
RUSSIAN-BORN AMERICAN PHILOSOPHER

Laws should be like clothes. They should be made to fit the people they are meant to serve.

CLARENCE DARROW,
AMERICAN LAWYER AND WRITER

Law is order, and good law is good order.

ARISTOTLE,
4TH-CENTURY B.C. GREEK PHILOSOPHER

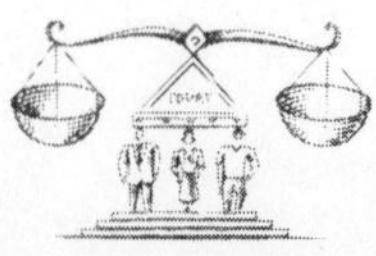

The law is a sort of hocus-pocus science that smiles in yer face while it picks yer pocket.

CHARLES MACKLIN,
17TH-CENTURY IRISH ACTOR AND DRAMATIST

Law and order are always and everywhere the law and order which protect the established hierarchy.

HERBERT MARCUSE,
GERMAN-BORN AMERICAN PHILOSOPHER

Men have feelings but the law does not.

NAPOLEON I,
EMPEROR OF FRANCE

Law is a majestic edifice, sheltering all of us, each stone of which rests on another.

JOHN GALSWORTHY,
ENGLISH WRITER AND DRAMATIST

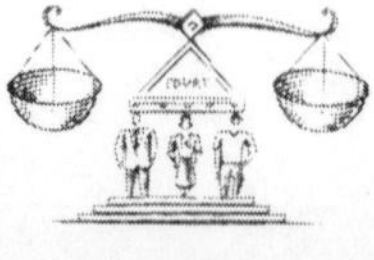

The law is the true embodiment of everything that's excellent.

WILLIAM S. GILBERT, ENGLISH POET AND WRITER

A law can be both economic folly and constitutional.

ANTONIN SCALIA, SUPREME COURT JUSTICE

Law is the harmony of the world.

RICHARD HOOKER, 16TH-CENTURY ENGLISH THEOLOGIAN

The law is so phallic! It doesn't leave much room for sensitivity, which must be why so many guys are happy in it.

ALYSON SINGER, AMERICAN LAWYER

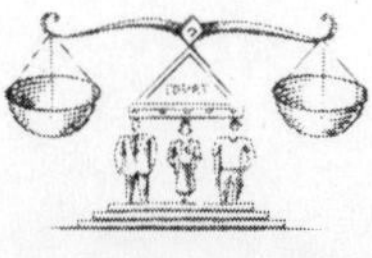

Law is experience developed by reason
and applied continually to further experience.

ROSCOE POUND,
DEAN EMERITUS, HARVARD LAW SCHOOL

The law is not majestic. The law is what public opinion says it is. I could tell you a lot about the law. . . . We got a man to argue for me tomorrow who wouldn't have me to dinner in his house. He talks on the phone with the President. But I have paid his price and he will be at my side for as long as it takes.

DUTCH SCHULTZ,
NOTORIOUS DEPRESSION-ERA MOBSTER,
IN E. L. DOCTOROW'S BILLY BATHGATE

Law is the backbone which keeps man erect.

S. C. YUTER,
AMERICAN JOURNALIST AND WRITER

The Law is good, if a man use it lawfully.

I TIMOTHY, 1:8

Law is but a heathen word for power.

DANIEL DEFOE,
17TH-CENTURY ENGLISH WRITER

The law is reason free from passion.

ARISTOTLE,
4TH-CENTURY B.C. GREEK PHILOSOPHER

The law will never make men free;
it is men who have got to make the law free.

HENRY DAVID THOREAU,
19TH-CENTURY AMERICAN WRITER

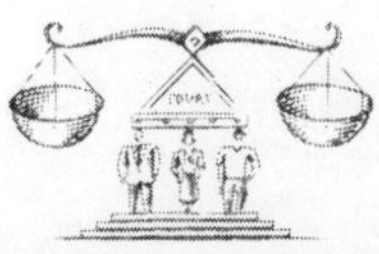

The more laws, the more offenders.

THOMAS FULLER,
17TH-CENTURY ENGLISH WRITER

The laws of a nation form the most instructive portion of its history.

EDWARD GIBBON,
18TH-CENTURY ENGLISH HISTORIAN

Woman throughout the ages has been mistress to the law, as man has been its master.

FREDA ADLER,
AMERICAN EDUCATOR

The law sees and treats women the way men see and treat women.

CATHARINE MACKINNON,
AMERICAN LAW PROFESSOR, FEMINIST, AND WRITER

It usually takes a hundred years to make a law, and then, after it has done its work, it usually takes a hundred years to get rid of it.

HENRY WARD BEECHER,
19TH-CENTURY AMERICAN CLERGYMAN

The law can never make us as secure as we are when we do not need it.

ALEXANDER M. BICKEL,
ROMANIAN-BORN AMERICAN LEGAL SCHOLAR

The criminal law represents the pathology of civilization.

MORRIS COHEN,
RUSSIAN-BORN AMERICAN PHILOSOPHER

Laws too gentle are seldom obeyed; too severe, seldom executed.

BENJAMIN FRANKLIN,
18TH-CENTURY AMERICAN STATESMAN AND PHILOSOPHER

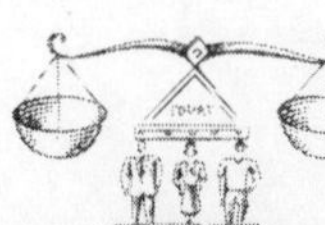

I know no method to secure the repeal of
bad or obnoxious laws so effective as
their stringent execution.

ULYSSES S. GRANT,
18TH PRESIDENT OF THE UNITED STATES

A strict observance of the written laws is
doubtless one of the high virtues of a good citizen,
but it is not the highest. The laws of necessity,
of self-preservation, of saving our country
when in danger, are of higher obligation.

THOMAS JEFFERSON,
3RD PRESIDENT OF THE UNITED STATES

It is difficult to make our material condition
better by the best laws, but it is easy
enough to ruin it by bad laws.

THEODORE ROOSEVELT,
26TH PRESIDENT OF THE UNITED STATES

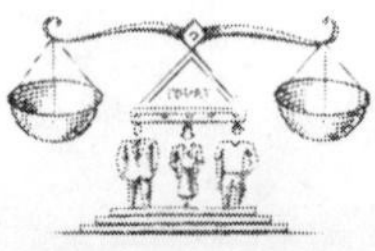

Many laws as certainly make bad men,
as bad men make many laws.

WALTER SAVAGE LANDOR,
18TH-CENTURY ENGLISH WRITER

Moral principle is the foundation of law.

RONALD D. DWORKIN,
LAW PROFESSOR, NEW YORK UNIVERSITY

A multitude of laws in a country is like
a great number of physicians,
a sign of weakness and malady.

VOLTAIRE,
18TH-CENTURY FRENCH WRITER

The best law leaves the least
discretion to the judge.

LATIN PROVERB

The laws put the safety of all
above the safety of one.

CICERO,
2ND-CENTURY B.C. ROMAN STATESMAN,
ORATOR, AND WRITER

The purpose of law is to prevent the strong
from always having their way.

OVID,
1ST-CENTURY ROMAN POET

As physicians are the preservers of the sick,
so are the laws of the injured.

EPICTETUS,
4TH-CENTURY B.C. GREEK PHILOSOPHER

Every law which originated in ignorance
and malice, and gratifies the passions from which
it sprang, we call the wisdom of our ancestors.

SYDNEY SMITH,
19TH-CENTURY ENGLISH WRITER

Laws are inherited like diseases.

JOHANN WOLFGANG VON GOETHE,
18TH-CENTURY GERMAN POET AND DRAMATIST

No laws, however stringent, can make the idle industrious, the thriftless provident, or the drunken sober.

SAMUEL SMILES,
19TH-CENTURY ENGLISH WRITER

Men would be great criminals did they need as many laws as they make.

LORD C. J. DARLING,
19TH-CENTURY ENGLISH JUDGE

When men are pure, laws are useless; when men are corrupt, laws are broken.

BENJAMIN DISRAELI,
19TH-CENTURY BRITISH PRIME MINISTER

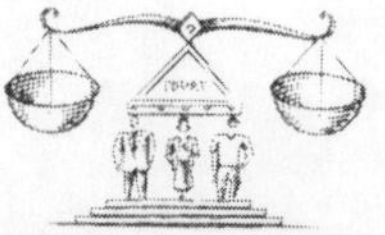

Someone has tabulated that we have 35 million laws on the books to enforce the ten commandments.

BERT MASTERSON

Laws are spider webs; they hold the weak and delicate who are caught in their meshes, but are torn in pieces by the rich and powerful.

ANACHARSIS,
1ST-CENTURY B.C. SCYTHIAN PHILOSOPHER

Law is certain in meaning, just in precept, convenient in execution, agreeable to the form of government, and productive of virtue in those that live under it.

FRANCIS BACON,
16TH-CENTURY ENGLISH PHILOSOPHER AND WRITER

Laws are not made for a righteous man, but for the lawless and disobedient, for the ungodly and for sinners.

I TIMOTHY, 1:9

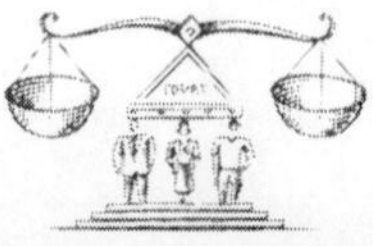

Postulating on the Predominating Principles of Pollution

In his opinion in a 1974 case involving the dumping of garbage in an unauthorized area, Georgia Appellate Judge H. Sol Banks proved he was an avid alliterationist. He wrote:

"Preventing public pollution permits promiscuous perusal of personality but persistent perspicacious patron persuasively provided pertinent perdurable preponderating presumption precedent preventing prison."

In other words, the defendant was found not guilty.

When No Means No

In a 1973 decision involving school segregation in Denver, Supreme Court Justice William J. Brennan Jr. achieved great notoriety among fellow jurists. It wasn't for his opinion, but for his penning of the Court's first quadruple negative sentence. He wrote:

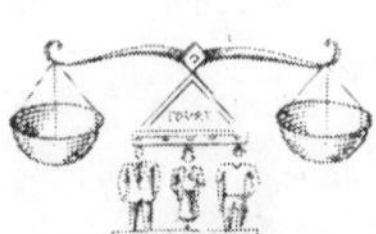

"This is not to say, however, that the prima facie case may not be met by evidence supporting a finding that a lesser degree of segregated schooling in the core city area would not have resulted even if the Board had not acted as it did."

A Great Judge of Weather

Samuel King, a U.S. District Court Judge in California, was annoyed that bad weather was keeping people from showing up for jury duty.

On February 18, 1986, he decreed: "I hereby order that it cease raining by Tuesday." California then suffered five years of drought.

So in 1991, he issued another decree: "I hereby rescind my order of February 18, 1986, and order that rain shall fall in California beginning February 27, 1991."

Days later, the state was hit by its heaviest rains in ten years.

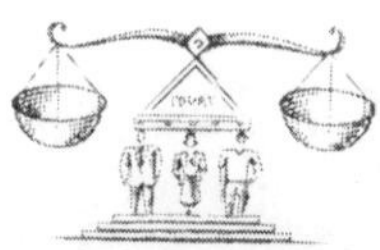

From Here to Eternity

A lease offered by a South Florida shopping center developer contains the following "End of the World" clause:

"If the end of the world is imminent before all Tenant's obligations are fully performed, then Landlord may elect to declare all rents to the end of the term to be immediately due and payable in full and may be enforced against Tenant by any available procedure. For remedial purposes, Landlord will be deemed aligned with the forces of light, and Tenant with forces of darkness, regardless of the parties' actual ultimate destinations, unless and until Landlord elects otherwise in writing."

LAWYERS

A lawyer's relationship to justice and wisdom . . . is on a par with a piano tuner's relationship to a concert. He neither composes the music, nor interprets it—he merely keeps the machinery running.

LUCILLE KALLEN,
20TH-CENTURY WRITER

Lawyers are . . . operators of the toll bridge across which anyone in search of justice must pass.

JANE BRYANT QUINN,
AMERICAN JOURNALIST

Being a lawyer is about serving justice. That's not only our greatest calling, it's our only calling.

ELLIS RUBIN,
AMERICAN LAWYER

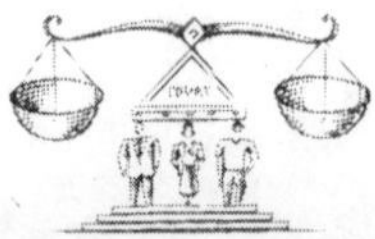

The lawyer's job in practice is to be on one hand the impassioned representative of his client to the world, and on the other the wise representative to his client of the legal system and the society, explaining and upholding the demands and restrictions that system places on them both.

SCOTT TUROW,
AMERICAN LAWYER AND WRITER

To be an effective criminal defense counsel, an attorney must be prepared to be demanding, outrageous, irreverent, blasphemous, a rogue, a renegade, and a hated, isolated, and lonely person . . . few love a spokesman for the despised and the damned.

CLARENCE DARROW,
AMERICAN LAWYER AND WRITER

Most good lawyers live well, work hard, and die poor.

DANIEL WEBSTER,
18TH-CENTURY AMERICAN STATESMAN, ORATOR, AND LAWYER

A personal injury lawyer is in a position to level the playing field and help people under our legal system.

PHILIP CORBOY,
AMERICAN LAWYER

The trial lawyer does what Socrates was executed for: making the worse argument appear the stronger.

IRVING R. KAUFMAN,
U.S. COURT OF APPEALS JUDGE

Law is a profession which abounds with honorable men, and in which there are fewer scamps than in any other.

GEORGE BORROW,
19TH-CENTURY ENGLISH WRITER AND LINGUIST

Only painters and lawyers can change white to black.

JAPANESE PROVERB

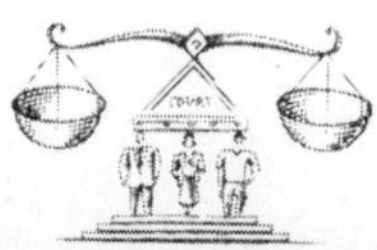

A good lawyer has a grasp of what yesterday teaches us about today and tomorrow, and knows that the real meaning of words like "freedom" or "justice" can only be found in the tapestry of history.

SOL M. LINOWITZ,
AMERICAN LAWYER

Anyone who believes a better day dawns when lawyers are eliminated bears the burden of explaining who will take their place. Who will protect the poor, the injured, the victims of negligence, the victims of racial discrimination and the victims of racial violence?

JOHN J. CURTIN, JR.,
AMERICAN LAWYER

I've never met a litigator who didn't think he was winning—right up until the moment the guillotine dropped.

WILLIAM F. BAXTER,
ASSISTANT U.S. ATTORNEY GENERAL

You cannot live without the lawyers,
and certainly you cannot die without them.

JOSEPH H. CHOATE,
AMERICAN LAWYER AND DIPLOMAT

A lawyer is a learned gentleman who rescues
your estate from your enemies and keeps it himself.

LORD HENRY PETER BROUGHAM,
18TH-CENTURY SCOTTISH JUDGE AND POLITICAL LEADER

I am not so afraid of lawyers as I used to be.
They are lambs in wolves' clothing.

EDNA ST. VINCENT MILLAY,
AMERICAN POET

The animals are not as stupid as one thinks—
they have neither doctors nor lawyers.

L. DOCQUIER,
FRENCH APHORIST

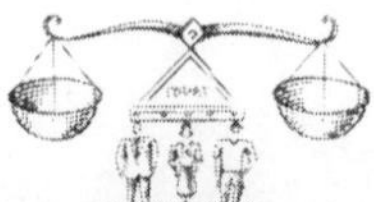

My daddy is a movie actor, and sometimes he plays the good guy, and sometimes he plays the lawyer.

MALCOLM FORD,
ON WHAT HIS FATHER, ACTOR HARRISON FORD, DOES FOR A LIVING

Show me your briefs and I'll show you mine.

PLJ,
SEEKING "AN ATTRACTIVE, SLIM & WITTY SINGLE WHITE FEMALE LAWYER, 25–30, FOR 'COURT-SHIP,'" THROUGH "PERSONALS FOR PROFESSIONALS" IN *THE NEW YORK LAW JOURNAL*

Lawyers like to throw around jargon and flowery language because it makes them feel self-important and prestigious.

GEORGE HATHAWAY,
AMERICAN WRITER

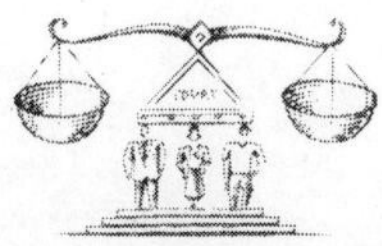

I don't know of any other industry, except the movie business, that has so many stars. Every lawyer thinks he's special.

PETER MORRISON,
AMERICAN LAWYER

No splints yet invented will heal a lawyer's broken reputation.

PAUL O'NEIL,
AMERICAN JOURNALIST AND WRITER

You want the unvarnished and ungarnished truth, and I'm no hand for that. I'm a lawyer.

MARY ROBERTS RINEHART,
AMERICAN WRITER

The New England folks have a saying, that three Philadelphia lawyers are a match for the very devil himself.

SALEM OBSERVER

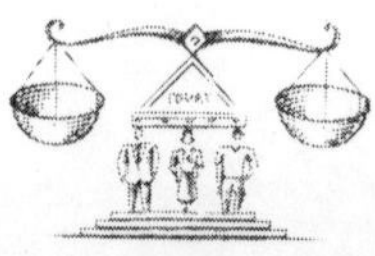

Lawyers take to politics like bears take to honey.

ROBERT TOWNSEND,
AMERICAN BUSINESSMAN

A peasant between two lawyers
is like a fish between two cats.

SPANISH PROVERB

What chance has the ignorant, uncultivated
liar against the educated expert?
What chance have I . . . against a lawyer?

MARK TWAIN,
AMERICAN WRITER AND HUMORIST

I have a high opinion of lawyers. With all their faults, they stack up well against those in every other occupation or profession. They are better to work with or play with or fight with or drink with than most other varieties of mankind.

HARRISON TWEED,
AMERICAN LAWYER

A lawyer with a briefcase can steal more than a hundred men with guns.

DON CORLEONE,
IN MARIO PUZO'S THE GODFATHER

I think we may class the lawyer in the natural history of monsters.

JOHN KEATS,
18TH-CENTURY ENGLISH POET

The best description of "utter waste" would be a busload of lawyers to go over a cliff with three empty seats.

LAMAR HUNT,
OWNER, KANSAS CITY CHIEFS FOOTBALL TEAM

A lawyer without history or literature is a mechanic, a mere working mason.

SIR WALTER SCOTT,
18TH-CENTURY SCOTTISH POET AND WRITER

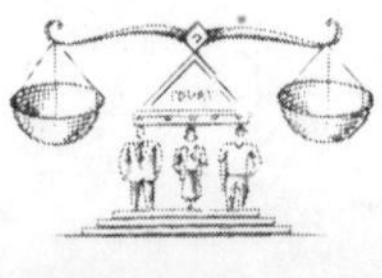

Why is there always a secret singing when a lawyer cashes in? Why does a hearse horse snicker hauling a lawyer away?

CARL SANDBURG,
AMERICAN WRITER

Lawyer: The only man in whom ignorance of the law is not punished.

ELBERT HUBBARD,
AMERICAN WRITER AND EDITOR

A lawyer's job is to manipulate the skeletons in other people's closets.

SOL STEIN,
AMERICAN BUSINESSMAN AND WRITER

When God wanted to chastise mankind, He invented lawyers.

RUSSIAN PROVERB

A lawyer's dream of heaven—every man reclaimed his property at the resurrection, and each tried to recover it from all his forefathers.

SAMUEL BUTLER,
19TH-CENTURY ENGLISH JOURNALIST AND WRITER

When there's a rift in the lute, the business of the lawyer is to widen the rift and gather the loot.

ARTHUR HAYS,
AMERICAN LAWYER

Lawyers use the law as shoemakers use leather: rubbing it, pressing it, and stretching it with their teeth, all to the end of making it fit for their purposes.

LOUIS XII,
KING OF FRANCE

If you can think of something which is connected with something without thinking of the something it is connected to, you have a legal mind.

THOMAS REED POWELL,
PROFESSOR, HARVARD UNIVERSITY

Some people think that a lawyer's business is to make white black; but his real business is to make white in spite of the stained and soiled condition which renders its true color questionable. He is simply an intellectual washing machine.

LOGAN E. BLECKLEY,
AMERICAN JUDGE

Lawyers are always more ready to get a man into troubles than out of them.

OLIVER GOLDSMITH,
18TH-CENTURY ENGLISH WRITER

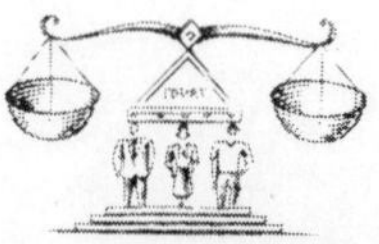

God works wonders now and then.
Behold: a lawyer, an honest man.

BENJAMIN FRANKLIN,
18TH-CENTURY AMERICAN STATESMAN AND PHILOSOPHER

Young lawyers attend the courts, not because they have business there but because they have no business anywhere else.

WASHINGTON IRVING,
18TH-CENTURY AMERICAN WRITER

The Devil makes his Christmas pie of lawyers' tongues.

ENGLISH PROVERB

Of course the cameras make some lawyers grandstand, but that's the way some lawyers are anyway. They talk for a living.

NANCY GRACE,
AMERICAN LAWYER

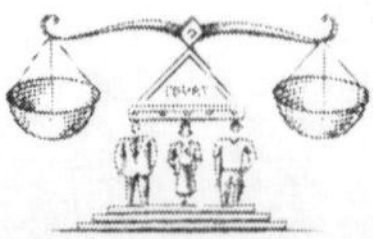

Mr. Attorney, I respect you, I fear you not;
and the less you speak of your own greatness,
the more I will think of it.

FRANCIS BACON,
ENGLISH PHILOSOPHER AND WRITER

No lawyer will ever go to Heaven so long
as there is room for more in Hell.

FRENCH PROVERB

I didn't become a lawyer because I like the law.
The law sucks. It's boring, but it can also be used
as a weapon. You want to bankrupt somebody?
Cost him everything he's worked for?
Make his wife leave him, even make his kids cry . . .
yeah, we can do that.

GREG GERMANN AS RICHARD FISH,
SENIOR PARTNER IN THE TELEVISION SHOW *ALLY MCBEAL*

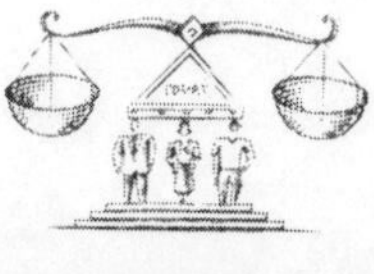

Lawyers have been and remain in the forefront of the battles to guarantee equality and justice for all Americans, and to enforce the protections of the Bill of Rights and the civil rights laws.

CHARISSE R. LILLIE,
CHAIR OF THE AMERICAN BAR ASSOCIATION COMMISSION ON OPPORTUNITIES FOR MINORITIES IN THE PROFESSION

Lawyer: One skilled in circumvention of the law.

AMBROSE BIERCE,
AMERICAN WRITER

The attitude of those of us who have anything to do with it [the law] should be that of the familiar sign in the western dance hall, "Don't shoot the piano player, he's doing the best he can."

WILLIAM L. PROSSER,
LEGAL SCHOLAR

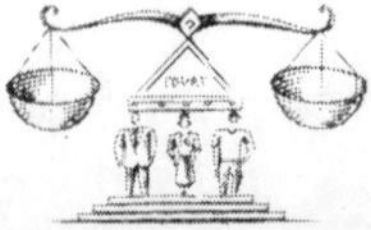

Lawyer: an individual whose principal role is
to protect his clients from others of his profession.

ANONYMOUS

There are three sorts of lawyers—
able, unable and lamentable.

ROBERT SMITH SURTEES,
19TH-CENTURY ENGLISH NOVELIST

The minute you read something you don't understand,
you can be almost sure it was drawn up by a lawyer.

WILL ROGERS,
AMERICAN HUMORIST

Old lawyers never die, they just lose their appeal.

ANONYMOUS

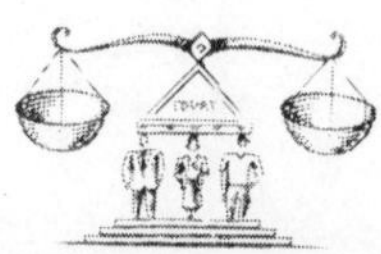

Whatever their failings as a class may be, and however likely to lose their immortal souls, lawyers do not generally lose papers.

ARTHUR TRAIN,
AMERICAN LAWYER AND WRITER

Lawyers: persons who write a 10,000-word document and call it a brief.

FRANZ KAFKA,
CZECHOSLOVAKIAN NOVELIST

It is a horrible demoralizing thing to be a lawyer. You look for such low motives in everyone and everything.

KATHERINE T. HINKSON,
IRISH POET AND WRITER

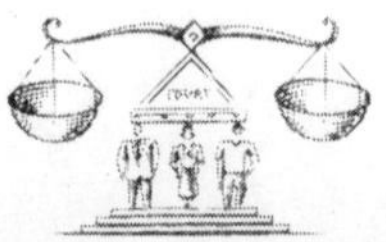

I happen to be dumb lucky because I grew up in a town where lawyers are people whom people look to for solutions. And who in their right mind, given that role, would not want to fulfill it?

DAVE SOUCY,
AMERICAN LAWYER

Lawyers, like bread, [are best] when they are young and new.

THOMAS FULLER,
17TH-CENTURY ENGLISH CLERGYMAN AND WRITER

A man without money needs no more fear a crowd of lawyers than a crowd of pickpockets.

WILLIAM WYCHERLEY,
17TH-CENTURY ENGLISH WRITER

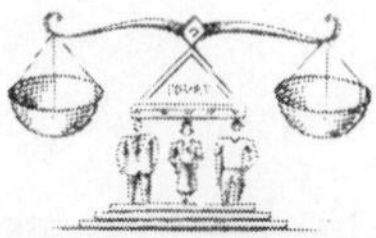

He saw a lawyer killing a viper
On a dunghill hard by his own stable,
And the Devil smiled, for it put him in mind
Of Cain and his brother Abel.

SAMUEL TAYLOR COLERIDGE,
18TH-CENTURY ENGLISH POET

A barrister of extended practice, if he has any talents at all, is the best companion in the world.

SIR WALTER SCOTT,
18TH-CENTURY SCOTTISH POET AND WRITER

The bar is still dominated by shortsightedness and self interest. Spotting change there is like watching a glacier move.

VERNON COUNTRYMAN,
PROFESSOR, HARVARD UNIVERSITY

Most lawyers are like whores. They serve the client who puts the highest fee on the table.

FLORYNCE RAE KENNEDY,
AMERICAN LAWYER AND CIVIL RIGHTS ACTIVIST

A lot of defense attorneys take the facts of the case and twist them around and try, in effect, to create a lie out of some truth.

JOHN KATZENBACH,
AMERICAN JOURNALIST

Lawyers and soldiers are the Devil's playmates.

FRENCH PROVERB

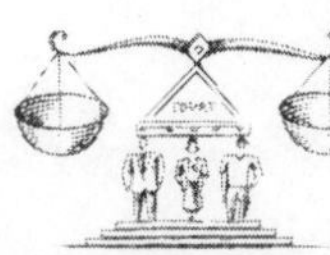

Attorneys are just good followers. . . .
The lawyer mentality is to follow the rules
and make a big pile doing it.

HARRY PALMER,
AMERICAN LAWYER

We are more casual about qualifying the people
we allow to act as advocates in the courtroom than
we are about licensing electricians.

WARREN BURGER,
SUPREME COURT JUSTICE

Most lawyers, it seems to me, simply can't balance
their energies: the goal of success and more
money chips away at them until they have succumbed
to a dangerous kind of myopia.

H. JAMES THOMAS,
AMERICAN LAWYER

Heaven Help Them

Attorney Rodney Donohoo, of Santa Ana, California, was riding up an elevator with two elderly women one day in 1990. One of the ladies asked if lawyers had offices on all the top floors of the building.

"Yes, they do," Donohoo replied.

"It's a good thing," the woman told her friend. "That's probably as close to heaven as most lawyers will ever get."

A Fool For a Client

In a 1985 criminal trial, Michael Blackwell, of Bridgeport, Connecticut, represented himself. At the end of the two-day trial, he was found guilty of two counts of attempted robbery by a jury that took less than a hour to deliberate.

As soon as the verdict was read, Blackwell told the judge he planned to appeal. When the judged asked him on what grounds, Blackwell replied, "I had an incompetent defense."

If At First You Don't Succeed . . .

In 1967, Maxcy Filer, then 36 years old and fresh out of law school, took the California bar exam for the first time.

He flunked the grueling three-day test. So he tried again . . . and again . . . and again. Twenty-four frustrating years later, Filer finally passed—on his forty-seventh try, at the age of 60.

"I never once thought seriously about giving up," he said.

What Gave Me Away?

Convicted con man Peter Horsford, who was accused of impersonating a lawyer, had trouble getting a trial date in New York in 1988.

The problem was that four of the judges considered for his trial were disqualified from hearing the case—because he had argued cases in their courtrooms.

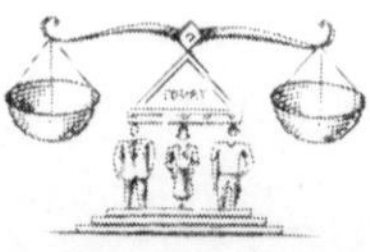

"I should have suspected he wasn't a lawyer," said one of the judges. "He was always so punctual and polite."

Legal Briefs

Miami lawyer Alvin Goodman showed up at the Metropolitan Correctional Center early one Sunday in 1989 to see a client. But because the attorney was violating the dress code by wearing shorts, he was denied entry.

Rather than go all the way home, Goodman stopped off at a nearby garage sale. Although there were no pants, he bought a nice turquoise skirt. He put it on and returned to the correctional center.

When the guard balked, Goodman argued that if women wearing pants are allowed inside, then men wearing skirts should be, too. The guard reluctantly agreed.

Two Sides to Everything

In the 1920s, a plaintiff brought suit against the City of New York after he claimed to have been seriously in-jured from falling into an open manhole.

During his trial, Dr. Willard Parker, appearing as an expert witness for the plaintiff, testified that the plaintiff "had been so badly hurt that he could lie on only one side."

Where upon the city attorney joked, "I suppose, doctor, you mean he would make a very poor lawyer?"

When Worlds Collide

In 1988, attorney Becky Klemt of Laramie, Wyoming, wrote letters to several attorneys in California offering a job to collect child support for a client whose husband had moved to Los Angeles.

In declining the offer, lawyer Stephen Corris, who specializes in international trade, wrote Klemt, "Without sounding pretentious, my current retainer for cases is a flat

$100,000, with an additional charge of $1,000 an hour."

Klemt then fired off a letter back to Corris, saying in part, "Steve, I've got news—you can't say you charge a $100,000 retainer fee and an additional $1,000 an hour without sounding pretentious. It just can't be done. Especially when you're writing to someone in Laramie, Wyoming, where you're considered pretentious if you wear socks to court or drive anything fancier than a Ford Bronco. Hell, Steve, all the lawyers in Laramie, put together, don't charge $1,000 an hour. . . .

"P.S.: Incidentally, we have advised our client of your hourly rate. She is willing to pay you $1,000 per hour to collect this judgment, provided it doesn't take you more than four seconds."

In the Name of Love

Seattle attorney Jeffrey Leppo was relieved when the judge granted his motion for a postponement of a case he was to argue in federal court in 1991.

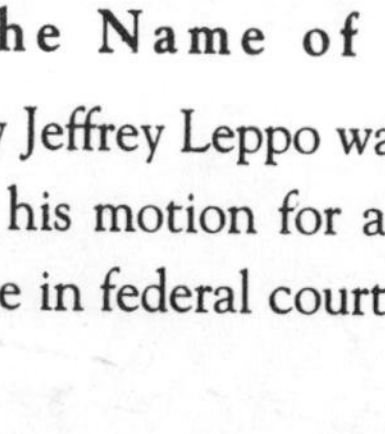

But then to his shock, the lawyer realized that the new date of the trial fell during his honeymoon. So Leppo filed a motion for a second postponement. Without it, he feared, there might not even be a wedding, let alone a honeymoon. Said Leppo in his motion, "It has taken counsel over thirty-four years to find someone whom he loves and who loves him."

A sympathetic judge granted the motion, and Leppo's wedding went off without a hitch.

CLIENT

Client, n.: A person who has made the customary choice between the two methods of being legally robbed.

AMBROSE BIERCE,
AMERICAN WRITER

If you're a litigating attorney, always discuss tactics with the client at the trial. Not only will this surprise your adversary but your client as well.

ARTHUR GREEBLER,
AMERICAN LAWYER

I'd rather have my hand cut off than betray the interests of a client.

RAYMOND BURR,
AS TELEVISION LAWYER PERRY MASON

Definition of a lawyer's function: To protect his clients from being persuaded by persons whom they do not know to enter into contracts which they do not understand to purchase goods which they do not want with money which they have not got.

LORD WILFRID ARTHUR GREENE,
ENGLISH JUDGE

Praise the adversary. He is the catalyst by which you bill your client. Damn the client. He is your true enemy.

STEVEN J. KUMBLE,
AMERICAN LAWYER

About half the practice of a decent lawyer consists in telling would-be clients that they are damned fools and should stop.

ELIHU ROOT,
AMERICAN LAWYER AND STATESMAN

[The] ideal client is the very wealthy man in very great trouble.

JOHN STERLING, AMERICAN LAWYER

Don't try to instruct your lawyer. If you do, you've got the wrong lawyer.

JOHN T. NOLAN

An investigation is underway, and for the first time in my life I may actually have to stoop to retaining a lawyer. This is the end of something pure and good. Once a fellow breaks down and hires his first attorney, he has gone and booked himself passage aboard the hand basket to Hades.

TOM ROBBINS, AMERICAN WRITER

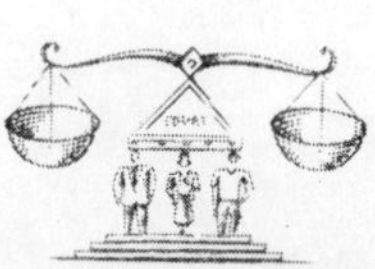

Of course people are getting smarter nowadays; they are letting lawyers instead of their conscience be their guides.

**WILL ROGERS,
AMERICAN ACTOR AND HUMORIST**

If there is any truth to the old proverb that "one who is his own lawyer has a fool for a client," the Court . . . now bestows a constitutional right on one to make a fool of himself.

**HARRY A. BLACKMUN,
SUPREME COURT JUSTICE, DISSENTING IN A 6-3 RULING THAT ALLOWED A DEFENDANT TO REFUSE COUNSEL**

Journalists are a hard group of people to love, but they're an easy group to defend.

**FLOYD ABRAMS,
AMERICAN LAWYER**

Chutzpa is that quality enshrined in a man who, having killed his mother and father, throws himself on the mercy of the court because he is an orphan.

LEO ROSTEN,
POLISH-AMERICAN WRITER

A defendant is entitled to a fair trial but not a perfect one.

U.S. SUPREME COURT

If there were no bad people there would be no good lawyers.

CHARLES DICKENS,
19TH-CENTURY ENGLISH WRITER

There is never a deed so foul that something couldn't be said for the guy; that's why there are lawyers.

MELVIN BELLI,
AMERICAN LAWYER

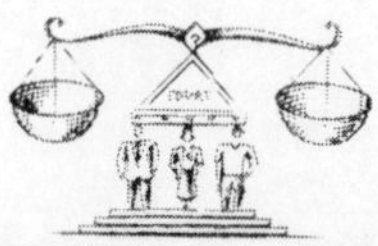

Things in law tend to be black and white.
But we all know that some people are a little bit guilty,
while other people are guilty as hell.

DONALD R. CRESSEY,
AMERICAN WRITER

I don't know if I want a lawyer to tell me what
I cannot do. I hire him to tell me how to
do what I want to do.

J.P. MORGAN,
AMERICAN FINANCIER

I get paid for seeing that my clients have every
break the law allows. I have knowingly
defended a number of guilty men. But the guilty
never escape unscathed. My fees are sufficient
punishment for anyone.

F. LEE BAILEY,
AMERICAN LAWYER

In former days, everyone found the assumption of innocence so easy; today we find fatally easy the assumption of guilt.

AMANDA CROSS,
AMERICAN LITERARY SCHOLAR AND WRITER

A woman has a much better chance than a man of acquittal on a murder charge. . . . If she happens to be a blonde, her chances rise about 45 percent.

JOHN MCGEORGE,
AUSTRALIAN PSYCHIATRIST

Fools and obstinate men make lawyers rich.

HENRY GEORGE BOHN,
19TH-CENTURY ENGLISH PUBLISHER

It took man thousands of years to put words down on paper, and his lawyers still wish he wouldn't.

MIGNON MCLAUGHLIN,
AMERICAN WRITER

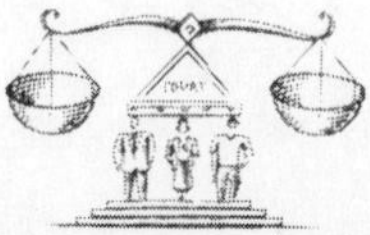

He who is always his own counselor will often have a fool for his client.

PORTFOLIO (A PHILADELPHIA MAGAZINE), AUGUST 1809

Most of my clients are chastened by having been caught, but often if they win the case, they think they are invincible.

ALAN DERSHOWITZ,
AMERICAN LAWYER AND HARVARD LAW PROFESSOR

When you're a lawyer, you expect your client to lie to you, but not when he is the president.

DICK HOUSER

It is easy to tell a lie, but hard to tell only one.

RICHARD WYDICK,
AMERICAN LAWYER ON CLIENTS WHO FIB

There seems to be a sense in America that we have a God-given right to be idiots and not have to pay for it.

CHARLES SYKES,
AMERICAN AUTHOR COMMENTING ON SUITS FILED BY PLAINTIFFS WHO WON'T ACCEPT BLAME FOR PROBLEMS THEY BROUGHT ON THEMSELVES

When you believe someone is truly innocent, then the job of defending them becomes more difficult because you know that you are the only thing between them and the jail house door.

RIKKI KLIEMAN,
AMERICAN LAWYER

As attorneys, we operate in a legal system where our stated purpose is to achieve justice for our clients. My clients, however, prefer victories over justice.

DANNY MANUASA,
AMERICAN LAWYER

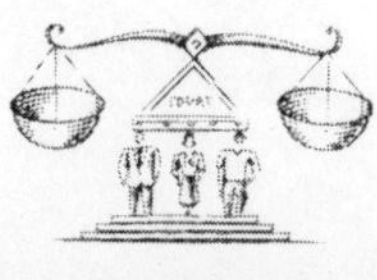

I'm trusting in the Lord and a good lawyer.

**OLIVER NORTH,
MARINE LT. COLONEL, BEFORE TESTIFYING
AT THE IRAN-CONTRA HEARINGS**

The Specialist

While working as a court-appointed attorney in Fulton County, Georgia, in 1991, Emory Potter was assigned a client who was accused of criminal trespass. During the pre-trial conference, Potter asked him if he had any prior arrests or convictions. "Yes, sir," the defendant admitted, lowering his eyes. "I've got quite a few."

"Any felonies?" Potter inquired.

"No, sir!" the defendant replied indignantly. "I specialize in misdemeanors!"

Preemptive Justice

Years ago in Kentucky, a prosecutor offered to settle the charge in a criminal case if the defendant would plead guilty and accept a five-year sentence.

On the advice of his defense attorney, the defendant turned down the deal. The case went to trial, where he was eventually convicted. Before imposing a life sentence without parole, the judged asked the defendant if he had anything to say.

"Yes, your honor," said the defendant. "You might as well tack on a few more years—because if I ever get out, I'm gonna kill my lawyer!"

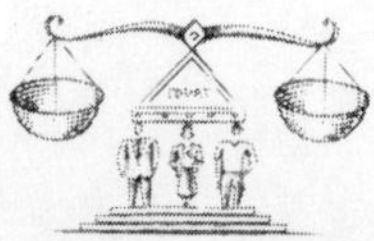

The Whole Truth and Nothing But

During a 1989 case in municipal court in Middletown, Ohio, a lawyer asked the judge to be excused from representing his client.

The judge scanned the courtroom, looking for a suitable replacement. But before he could find one, the defendant stood up and said, "That's all right, Judge. I won't be needing another lawyer. I've decided to tell the truth."

Once Bitten . . .

About a year after unsuccessfully defending a client, British lawyer Sir Patrick Hastings found himself cross-examining the very same man in another trial.

The witness was not being cooperative, so Sir Patrick, who did not realize the man was once his client, warned him, "You will answer my questions directly, take my advice."

"I will not take your advice, sir," the witness snapped. "I took it once and it put me inside [jail] for six months."

LAW FIRMS

The screening process through which law firms choose new partners is perhaps as well considered as anything this side of a papal election.

NEAL JOHNSTON,
CHIEF OF STAFF, NEW YORK CITY COUNCIL

Panic is a way of life in a major law firm, and clients like Sonny Capps can cause ulcers. Our clients are our only assets, so we kill ourselves for them.

LAWYER OLIVER LAMBERT,
IN JOHN GRISHAM'S THE FIRM

No one is under pressure. There wasn't a light on when I left at 2 o'clock this morning.

HOYT MOONE,
AMERICAN LAWYER

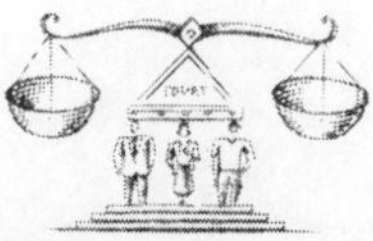

We shake papers at each other the way primitive tribes shake spears.

JOHN JAY OSBORN, JR., AUTHOR OF THE ASSOCIATES

I regret that I have but one law firm to give to my country.

ADLAI E. STEVENSON, AMERICAN LAWYER AND DIPLOMAT, REFERRING TO PRESIDENT JOHN KENNEDY'S REPEATED SELECTION OF MEMBERS OF STEVENSON'S LAW FIRM TO SERVE IN HIS ADMINISTRATION

Law firms are becoming like professional sports teams—the uniforms remain the same, but the players change regularly.

TERRY CARTER, AMERICAN JOURNALIST

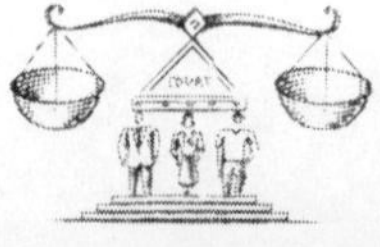

Law is one of the last citadels of wavering conservatism in an untidy world and the offices of most lawyers reflect it.

ROBERT TRAVER,
AMERICAN WRITER AND JUDGE

To compensate for minor irregularities in the earth's rotation, official international timekeepers add one second to this day. U.S. law firms adjust their bills.

DAVE BARRY,
AMERICAN SYNDICATED COLUMNIST,
ON THE ANNUAL TIME ADJUSTMENT

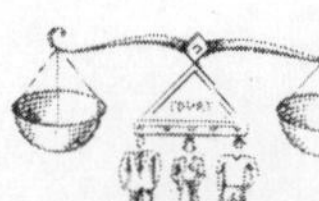

A No-Win Situation

At an annual Bosses Night dinner for lawyers sponsored by legal secretaries in Helena, Montana, it was time to announce the Boss of the Year. The master of ceremonies began: "First of all, our winner is a graduate of the University of Montana. So that already eliminates some of you as candidates. Our winner also is a partner in a downtown Helena law firm. That eliminates some more of you. Our nominee is honest, upright, dedicated . . ."

A voice from the audience cut in: "Well, there go the rest of us."

At Least There's Free Parking

The following classified ad appeared in a 1989 issue of the *Texas Bar Journal*:

"Small, highly disorganized . . . law firm, having characteristically waited past the last minute, frantically seeks associate with two to four years of experience in general business representation and business litigation. Successful applicant must be able to function with little or no guidance in extremely chaotic environment, and be able to stand long periods of indecision punctuated by short bursts of frantic activity. . . . Toleration of tobacco smoke required. Affinity for hard liquor recommended. . . . Free parking. . . . Only the stouthearted need apply."

JUDGES

The judge weighs the arguments and puts a brave face on the matter, and, since there must be a decision, decides as he can, and hopes he has done justice.

RALPH WALDO EMERSON,
19TH-CENTURY AMERICAN WRITER AND POET

A judge is one more learned than witty, more reverend than plausible, and more advised than confident. Above all things, integrity is their portion and proper virtue.

FRANCIS BACON,
16TH-CENTURY ENGLISH PHILOSOPHER AND WRITER

Appellate Division judges [are] the whores who became madams.

MARTIN ERDMANN,
AMERICAN LAWYER

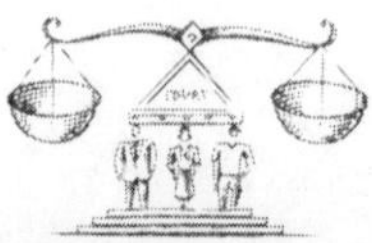

The right to one's day in court is meaningless if the judge who hears the case lacks the talent, experience and temperament that will enable him to protect imperiled rights and to render a fair decision.

WILLIAM H. REHNQUIST,
SUPREME COURT JUSTICE

Judges are, in many respects, like parents. You have to give them a good enough reason to do what you want.

DARLENE RICKER,
AMERICAN LAWYER AND LEGAL JOURNALIST

When did a judge ever think? He's paid not to.

MAXWELL ANDERSON, AMERICAN PLAYWRIGHT,
AND HAROLD HICKERSON, AMERICAN WRITER

It has been said that a judge is a member of the Bar who once knew a governor.

CURTIS BOK,
PENNSYLVANIA SUPREME COURT JUSTICE

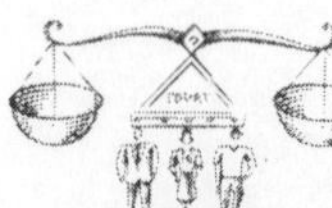

Judges are the weakest link in our system of justice, and they are also the most protected.

ALAN DERSHOWITZ,
LAWYER AND HARVARD LAW PROFESSOR

For Heaven's sake discard the monstrous wig which makes the English judges look like rats peeping through bunches of oakum.

THOMAS JEFFERSON,
3RD PRESIDENT OF THE UNITED STATES

The ability of a judge to put himself into the shoes of the men and women who appear before him is the heart of being a decent judge.

JOSEPH A. WAPNER,
JUDGE OF THE TELEVISION SHOW THE PEOPLE'S COURT

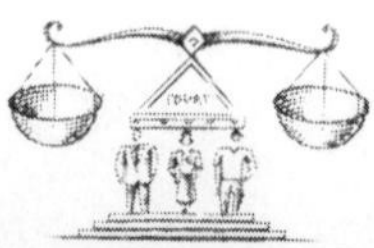

Courtrooms contain every symbol of authority that a set designer could imagine. Everyone stands up when you come in. You wear a costume identifying you as, if not quite divine, someone special.

IRVING R. KAUFMAN,
U.S. COURT OF APPEALS JUDGE

A judge is unjust who hears but one side of a case, even though he decides it justly.

SENECA,
1ST-CENTURY B.C. ROMAN STATESMAN
AND PHILOSOPHER

I'll have you understand I am running this court, and the law hasn't got a damn thing to do with it!

SAMUEL ERVIN, JR.,
UNITED STATES SENATOR,
RECALLING AN OLD MAGISTRATE'S
WORDS TO A YOUNG ATTORNEY

There are no more reactionary people in the world than judges.

NIKOLAI LENIN,
RUSSIAN REVOLUTIONARY LEADER

There should be many judges, for few will always do the will of few.

NICCOLO MACHIAVELLI,
15TH-CENTURY ITALIAN STATESMAN AND POLITICAL PHILOSOPHER

Judge: A law student who marks his own examination papers.

H. L. MENCKEN,
AMERICAN JOURNALIST

The thing to fear is not the law but the judge.

RUSSIAN SAYING

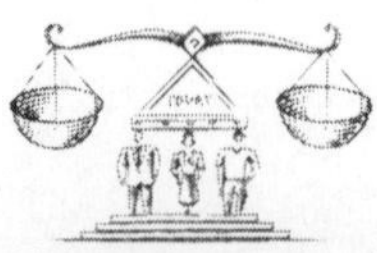

The judge is condemned when the guilty is acquitted.

PUBLILIUS SYRUS,
1ST-CENTURY B.C. ROMAN WRITER

The acme of judicial distinction means the ability to look a lawyer straight in the eyes for two hours and not hear a damned word he says.

JOHN MARSHALL,
SUPREME COURT JUSTICE

The halls of justice. That's the only place you see the justice, is in the halls.

LENNY BRUCE,
AMERICAN COMEDIAN

Judging is a lonely job in which a man is, as near as may be, an island entire.

ABE FORTAS,
SUPREME COURT JUSTICE

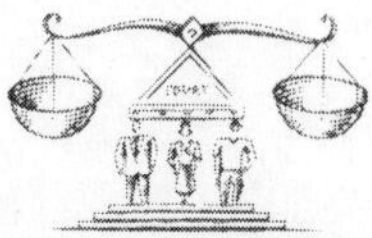

I don't want to know what the law is,
I want to know who the judge is.

ROY M. COHN,
AMERICAN LAWYER

Judges are best in the beginning;
they deteriorate as time passes.

TACITUS,
1ST-CENTURY ROMAN HISTORIAN

A judge is merely a lawyer who has been benched.

CHARLES E. CLARK,
U.S. COURT OF APPEALS JUDGE

Knowing that religion does not furnish
grosser bigots than law,
I expect little from old judges.

THOMAS JEFFERSON,
3RD PRESIDENT OF THE UNITED STATES

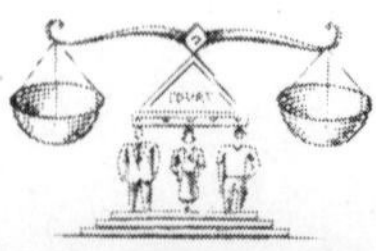

The law is relaxed when the judge shows pity.

PUBLILIUS SYRUS,
1ST-CENTURY B.C. ROMAN WRITER

A good and faithful judge prefers what is right to what is expedient.

HORACE,
1ST-CENTURY B.C. ROMAN POET AND SATIRIST

He who has the judge for his father goes into court with an easy mind.

MIGUEL DE CERVANTES,
16TH-CENTURY SPANISH WRITER

The duty of a judge is to render justice; his art is to delay it.

JEAN DE LA BRUYÈRE,
17TH-CENTURY FRENCH WRITER AND MORALIST

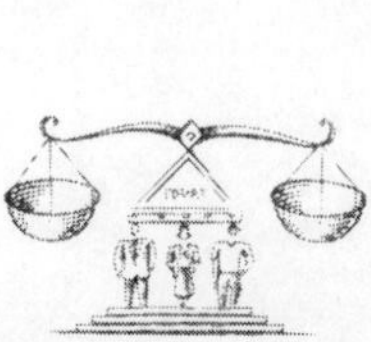

The judge is nothing but the law speaking.

BENJAMIN WHICHCOTE,
17TH-CENTURY ENGLISH PHILOSOPHICAL THEOLOGIAN

Judges are apt to be naive, simple-minded men.

OLIVER WENDELL HOLMES JR.,
SUPREME COURT JUSTICE

I will tell you about judges. You can take the most mild-mannered and tender-hearted man you ever saw, make him a judge for life, and his disposition to tyrannize over people will grow with what he feeds on.

CHAMP CLARK,
UNITED STATES CONGRESSMAN

A lifetime diet of the law alone turns judges into dull, dry husks.

WILLIAM O. DOUGLAS,
SUPREME COURT JUSTICE

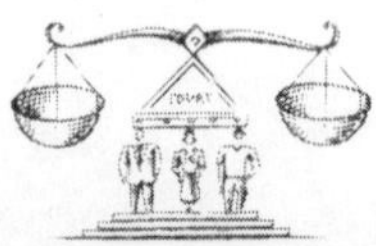

A judge should be about sixty, clean shaven, with white hair, china-blue eyes, and suffer from hemorrhoids so that he will have that concerned look.

ANONYMOUS

I'm surprised [the judge] doesn't just take out a rifle in the courtroom and shoot 'em.

LESLIE ABRAMSON,
DEFENSE ATTORNEY IN THE MURDER TRIAL OF ERIK AND LYLE MENENDEZ ASSERTING THAT THE JUDGE WAS BIASED

I always approach Judge [Lemuel] Shaw as a savage approaches his fetish, knowing that he is ugly, but feeling that he is great.

RUFUS CHOAK,
19TH-CENTURY AMERICAN JURIST

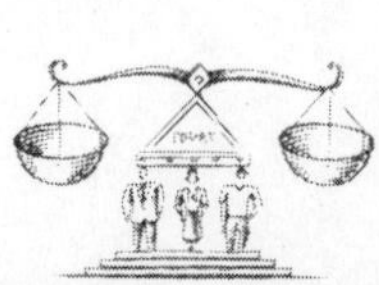

I'm a mere flash in the pan. I take solace in the fact that nobody remembers who the judge was in the Lindbergh case, the William Kennedy Smith case, the Mike Tyson case. . . . This will all pass.

LANCE ITO,
JUDGE IN THE O.J. SIMPSON TRIAL

Judge:
n. Ringmaster
v. To toss a coin

ROBERT J. MORRIS,
AMERICAN LAWYER

A judge is not free, like a loose cannon, to inflict indiscriminate damage whenever he announces that he is acting in his judicial capacity.

POTTER STEWART,
SUPREME COURT JUSTICE

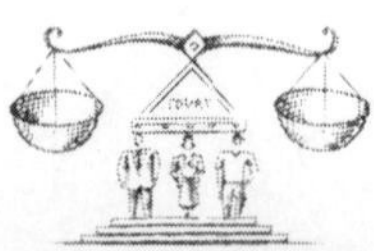

All in all I'd rather have been a judge than a miner. And what's more, being a miner, as soon as you are too old and tired and sick and stupid to do the job properly, you have to go. Well, the very opposite applies with judges.

PETER COOK,
BRITISH WRITER AND ENTERTAINER

Go Ahead . . . Make My Day

When two attorneys vehemently argued over a motion in her courtroom in 1992, Providence (Rhode Island) Superior Court Judge Patricia Hurst threatened to shoot them both—with a water pistol.

"I told them I have a good way of dealing with prolonged motions," the squirt-gun-toting judge told reporters later.

Because she was seen brandishing the squirt gun in court, Hurst was suspended for a month. Said Hurst, who surrendered the water gun to her attorney, "I'm probably guilty of having a bad sense of humor."

A Time To Rhyme

Michigan Appellate Court Judge John H. Gillis was so inspired by Joyce Kilmer's classic poem "Trees," that he wrote this verse in a 1983 opinion:

We thought that we would never see
A suit to compensate a tree.
A suit whose claim in tort is prest
Upon a mangled tree's behest;
A tree whose battered trunk was prest
Against a Chevy's crumpled crest;
A tree that faces each new day
With bark and limb in disarray;
A tree that may forever bear
A lasting need for tender care.
Flora lovers though we three,
We must uphold the court's decree.
Affirmed.

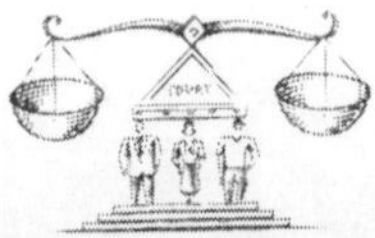

A Fine(d) Judge

An Alaskan judge levied a $500 fine on someone he knew better than anyone else—himself!

In 1991, Magistrate Craig McMahon of Bethel was swamped with 150 more cases than he had the previous year. To make matters worse, he had no secretary or computer. He had to write his decisions on an old typewriter.

Cases piled up and a few got lost on his desk. As a result, two alcohol prosecution cases had to be dismissed because McMahon had not scheduled speedy trials. "I felt pretty bad about losing the cases because of my procrastination," said the magistrate. "So I fined myself."

Short and Sweet

In 1990, Buffalo attorney Leonard Brizdle was arguing a case before New York Supreme Court Judge Carlton Fisher who called for briefs in ten days.

"Judge," said Brizdle, "if you can give me more time, I can write a shorter brief."

Declared Judge Fisher, "Briefs in twenty days!"

And Pick Up Your Socks While You're At It

San Francisco Superior Court Judge Lucy Kelly McCabe often answers her own phone when it rings in chambers. Sometimes she wishes she hadn't.

That's because she occasionally receives an earful from chauvinist lawyers who verbally abuse her on the assumption that she is a lowly law clerk.

One day in 1992, Judge McCabe answered her phone and was given a tongue-lashing from an attorney who thought he was talking to her law clerk. He had just found out his case was taken off the calendar because a declaration wasn't signed. "Why didn't you call me?" he demanded.

"Because we're not your mother," snapped Judge McCabe before hanging up.

Bathroom Humor

When Maine Superior Court Justice Francis C. Marsano stepped into the bathroom off his chambers one memorable day in 1993, he heard an unusual click as the door closed behind him. The pin attached to the door handle that moves the bolt had broken.

No courthouse workers discovered Marsano before leaving for the day. Because the bathroom was windowless and concrete-walled, the judge was forced to spend the night there, sleeping on rolls of toilet paper.

After a clerk discovered Marsano's plight the next morning, workers used a sledgehammer to free the judge.

How did he view being locked in a courthouse bathroom for sixteen hours? Said Marsano, "It puts a whole different spin on 'judicial seclusion.'"

JURIES

Percy Foreman and I once had an argument as to which of us had picked the most stupid jury. I think I won with one that returned a verdict which amounted to "Not guilty with a recommendation of clemency because of reasonable doubt."

F. LEE BAILEY,
AMERICAN LAWYER

In the McFarland case the defendant set up the plea of insanity, and succeeded in proving himself a fool. And he was acquitted by a jury of his peers.

AMBROSE BIERCE,
AMERICAN WRITER

If the district attorney wanted, a grand jury would indict a ham sandwich.

SYDNEY BIDDLE BARROWS,
"THE MAYFLOWER MADAM"

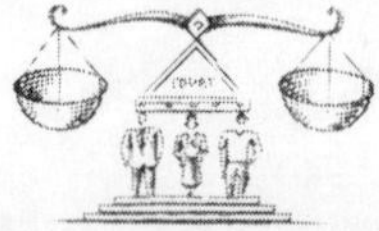

Today, the grand jury is the total captive of the prosecutor who, if he is candid, will concede that he can indict anybody, at any time, for almost anything, before any grand jury.

WILLIAM J. CAMPBELL,
U.S. DISTRICT COURT JUDGE

Juries . . . have the effect . . . of placing the control of the law in the hands of those who would be most apt to abuse it.

JAMES FENIMORE COOPER,
18TH-CENTURY AMERICAN WRITER

With attractive women [defendants] . . . juries sometimes have to be restrained from handing them a medal for their crimes.

JOHN MCGEORGE,
AUSTRALIAN PSYCHIATRIST

I never saw twelve men in my life, that,
if you could get them to understand a
human case, were not true and right.

CLARENCE DARROW,
AMERICAN LAWYER AND WRITER

A jury consists of twelve persons chosen to
decide who has the better lawyer.

ROBERT FROST,
AMERICAN POET

The average juror . . . wraps himself in civic
virtue. He's a judge now. He tries to act
the part and do the right thing.

JACOB D. FUCHSBERG,
PRESIDENT, AMERICAN TRIAL LAWYERS ASSOCIATION

Jury duty [is] a bog of quicksand on the path to justice.

SIDNEY BERNARD

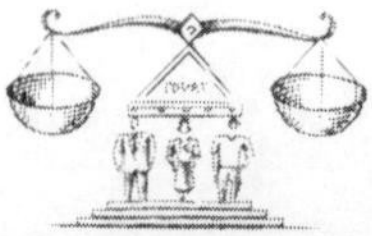

Jury: Twelve men of limited information and intelligence, chosen precisely because of their lack of intellectual resilience.

H. L. MENCKEN,
AMERICAN JOURNALIST

We have a criminal jury system which is superior to any in the world; and its efficiency is only marred by the difficulty of finding twelve men every day who don't know anything and can't read.

MARK TWAIN,
AMERICAN WRITER AND HUMORIST

In today's world a peer is not a hermit.

NEWTON MINOW,
FCC CHAIRMAN AND LAWYER,
ABOUT THE JUSTICE SYSTEM'S
PRACTICE OF EXCLUDING POTENTIAL
JURORS WHO FOLLOW THE NEWS

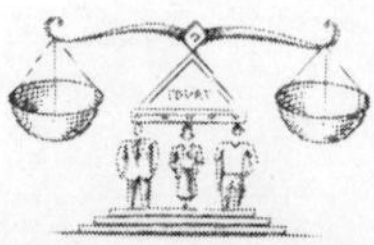

I would rather have my fate in the hands of twenty-three representative citizens of the county than in the hands of a politically appointed judge.

ROBERT MORGENTHAU,
NEW YORK CITY DISTRICT ATTORNEY,
DEFENDING THE SECRECY
OF GRAND JURY PROCEEDINGS

The jury is, above all, a political institution, and it must be regarded in this light in order to be duly appreciated.

ALEXIS DE TOCQUEVILLE,
19TH-CENTURY FRENCH STATESMAN AND WRITER

We, the jury, find our client not guilty.

VERDICT OF A JURY IN THE MUNICIPAL
COURT AT FORT SMITH, ARKANSAS,
IN A DRUNKENNESS CASE, DEC. 2, 1933

I have what jurors want. They want charisma. They want a fight in the courtroom. They don't want placidity. They don't want a one-dimensional lawsuit. They came here for a show. And they want to do what's right.

PHILIP CORBOY,
AMERICAN LAWYER

The jury is a collection of sedentary owls.

ELBERT HUBBARD,
AMERICAN WRITER AND EDITOR

A jury is a group of twelve people of average ignorance.

HERBERT SPENCER,
19TH-CENTURY ENGLISH PHILOSOPHER

It is the "ordinariness" of the jury that finally emerges as its unique strength.

MELVYN B. ZERMAN,
AMERICAN WRITER

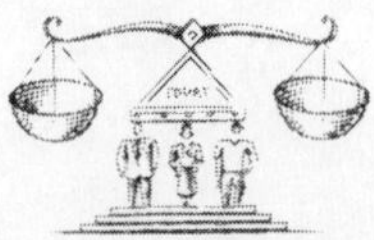

When you go into court you are putting your fate into the hands of twelve people who weren't smart enough to get out of jury duty.

NORM CROSBY,
AMERICAN COMEDIAN

Most often a jury reaches the right verdict even if it's for the wrong reasons.

RIKKI KLIEMAN,
AMERICAN LAWYER

"He said, she said" is enough to go to a jury. There are plenty of people making little rocks out of big rocks right now in the penitentiary on the basis of the jury believing "she said" and disbelieving "he said."

DANIEL POLSBY,
LAW PROFESSOR, NORTHWESTERN UNIVERSITY

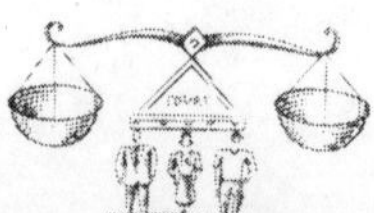

Excuses, Excuses . . .

People will say anything to escape jury duty. Here are a few of the wacky excuses actually uttered in court:

"I sneeze frequently and my false teeth fly out several feet in front of me, which might be distracting to the courtroom proceedings."

"Due to a bad case of bad breath, I would prefer not to be on jury duty, since I would hate to offend anyone."

"I work nights and I would not like listening to someone else's troubles during the morning hours."

"My diabetic poodle needs insulin shots twice a day."

"I am not God and neither are you. Thus, who are we to judge anyone else?"

Foolhardy

At the beginning of a trial in the Fourth Judicial District of Tennessee, the defendant stuck by his earlier plea of not guilty.

However, once the jury of eight women and four men was selected, the defendant switched his plea.

"Why the change?" the judge asked. "Were you persuaded to plead guilty?"

"No, your Honor," the defendant replied. "When I pleaded not guilty, I didn't know women would be on the jury. I can't fool one woman, so I know I can't fool eight of them."

Jury Prudence

Attorney Richard Glasson of Carson City, Nevada, was defending a 1989 slip-and-fall case in Douglas County District Court where the plaintiff's attorney was being especially annoying.

Just before the lunch recess, the jury sent out a note to the court which read: "We, the jury, in the interest of an expeditious trial, and for the general reduction of immaterial and repetitious questioning, do hereby recommend that a shocking collar device be securely fastened to plaintiff's counsel. The control of said device shall be entrusted to a responsible member of the jury panel to be selected following the next recess. We thank you for your support."

Plaintiff's counsel went out in the hall with Glasson and immediately settled the case.

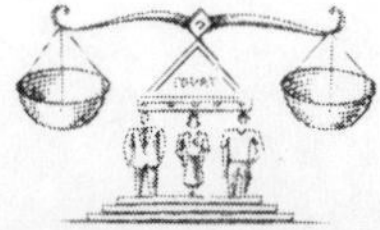

I'll Sleep on It

Judge Gerald Kalina of Hastings, Minnesota, was asking prospective jurors at the outset of a 1990 trial whether any of them had scheduling conflicts or illnesses that might prevent their serving that day.

One candidate raised his hand and said, "I suffer from narcolepsy and I'm worried that if I am chosen, I might nod off or fall asleep during part of the trial."

"Well, we can't have that," replied Kalina. "That's the job of the judge!"

WITNESSES

For a plot hatched in hell, don't expect angels for witnesses.

ROBERT PERRY, AMERICAN LAWYER

In response to the question: "Is that your conclusion that this man is a malingerer?" Dr. Unsworth responded: "I wouldn't be testifying if I didn't think so, unless I was on the other side, then it would be a post traumatic condition."

LADNER V. HIGGINS, 1954 LOUISIANA APPELLATE COURT

I think that one of the most fundamental responsibilities . . . is to give testimony in a court of law, to give it honestly and willingly.

ADLAI E. STEVENSON, AMERICAN LAWYER AND DIPLOMAT

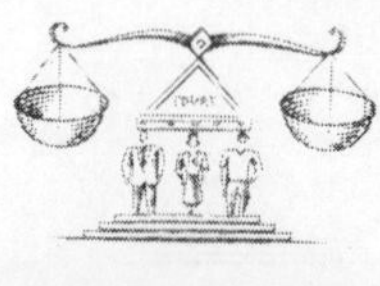

Lies and liars come in all types of packages. At some point the difference between an honest witness and a dishonest one is attitude. Honest witnesses remember the facts the way they must have been, dishonest witnesses remember them the way they should have been.

ERIC ZAGRANS,
AMERICAN LAWYER

If you talk to any lawyer who is honest, they'll tell you they think [unethical coaching] happens, and it happens a lot. It is a very easy thing to coach your witnesses. And if you have unscrupulous witnesses to begin with, that's the only nudge they need.

PORTIA MOORE,
AMERICAN LAWYER

Hold Onto Your Seat

During a trial at which Carl S. Black was an attorney, an eminent psychologist was called to testify. A severe, no-nonsense professional, she sat down in the witness chair, unaware that its rear legs were set precariously on the back of the raised platform. "Will you state your name?" asked the district attorney.

Tilting back in her chair, she opened her mouth to answer, but instead catapulted head-over-heels backward and landed in a stack of exhibits and recording equipment. Everyone watched in stunned silence as she extricated herself, rearranged her disheveled dress and hair, and was reseated on the witness stand. The glare she directed at onlookers dared anyone to so much as smirk.

"Well, Doctor," continued the district attorney, without changing expression, "we could start with an easier question."

Sleepy Heads

Phoenix lawyer Clint Batterton was trying to lighten his cross-examination of an anesthesiologist who was a plaintiff in a securities fraud case in 1988.

"I guess that means you and I are in the same business because we both put people to sleep," Batterton joked.

"Yes," replied the witness. "But I wake them up."

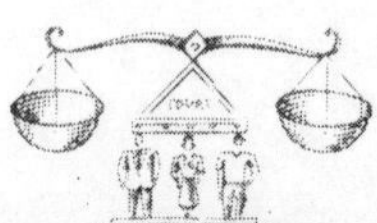

THE SUPREME COURT

Who is to say that five men ten years ago were right whereas five men looking the other direction today are wrong.

**HARRY A. BLACKMUN,
SUPREME COURT JUSTICE,
ON PRIOR CO'JRT DECISIONS,
ESPECIALLY 5-4 VOTES**

Something about our courtroom scares lawyers to death. Some fellows have fainted.

**WILLIAM J. BRENNAN, JR.,
SUPREME COURT JUSTICE**

If you took the brains of the majority of the Supreme Court and put them into the head of a bird, the bird would fly backward for ever and ever and ever.

**BENJAMIN HOOKS,
CHAIRMAN, NAACP**

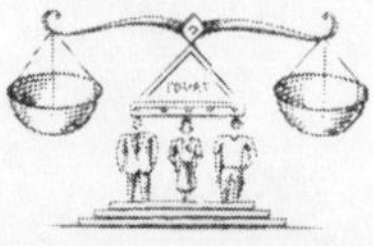

They were political animals before
they got to the Supreme Court, and they
don't change when they get there.

CHRISTINE KELLETT, LAW PROFESSOR, DICKINSON SCHOOL, COMMENTING THAT SUPREME COURT JUSTICES ARE IN STEP WITH THE POPULACE ON MOST ISSUES

You know, it's almost time to turn back the clock.
That's right, the Supreme Court's back in session.

JAY LENO, AMERICAN COMEDIAN

The people can change Congress but only God
can change the Supreme Court.

GEORGE W. NORRIS, UNITED STATES SENATOR

For the most part . . . we function as nine small
independent law firms.

LEWIS F. POWELL, JR., SUPREME COURT JUSTICE

We're all eccentrics. We're nine prima donnas.

HARRY A. BLACKMUN,
SUPREME COURT JUSTICE

We current justices read the Constitution in the only way that we can—as 20th-century Americans.

WILLIAM J. BRENNAN, JR.,
SUPREME COURT JUSTICE

If this country wanted its Supreme Court to reflect the immediate social or political wishes of the nation's people, it would provide for the election of the court. And if the founding fathers had wanted it that way, they could have said so—or at least hinted at it. They did just the opposite. They designed a system that tried to immunize the court from the changing moods and passions of the people.

MARIO CUOMO,
AMERICAN POLITICIAN

Our Constitution was not written in the sands to be washed away by each wave of new judges blown in by each successive political wind.

HUGO L. BLACK,
SUPREME COURT JUSTICE

In an era of "sound bites" and instant opinion polls it is dangerous to apply broad labels to a single [Supreme Court] term.

LEWIS F. POWELL, JR.,
SUPREME COURT JUSTICE

One puts on black robes to scare the hell out of white people, while the other puts on white robes to scare the hell out of blacks.

MORRIS K. UDALL,
UNITED STATES CONGRESSMAN,
CONTRASTING SUPREME COURT JUSTICES
AND KU KLUX KLAN MEMBERS

Whenever you put a man on the Supreme Court
he ceases to be your friend.

HARRY S TRUMAN,
33RD PRESIDENT OF THE UNITED STATES

Books? Who Needs Books?

When the Supreme Court was moved from the old capital of Philadelphia to Washington, D.C., in 1800, the government failed to provide the justices with law books.

Said Robert H. Jackson, author of *The Supreme Court in the American System of Government*, "[That] accounts for the high quality of early opinions."

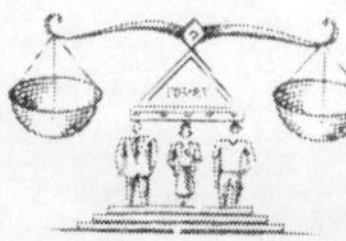

CODES OF CONDUCT

ETHICS

Lawyers know that no other group or profession sets higher ethical standards, disciplines itself so rigorously, [and] contributes so much unpaid service to the public.

DAVID R. BRINK,
PRESIDENT, AMERICAN BAR ASSOCIATION

Nobody has a more sacred obligation to obey the law than those who make the law.

SOPHOCLES,
5TH-CENTURY B.C. GREEK DRAMATIST

I didn't really mean that all lawyers are dishonest. Just that the honest ones are all poor.

ANN GERBER,
AMERICAN JOURNALIST

An eminent lawyer cannot be a dishonest man. Tell me a man is dishonest, and I will answer he is no lawyer. He cannot be, because he is careless and reckless of justice; the law is not in his heart [and] . . . is not the standard and rule of his conduct.

DANIEL WEBSTER,
18TH-CENTURY AMERICAN STATESMAN,
ORATOR, AND LAWYER

If young people entering the law are honest with themselves, have the ability to say no, resolve not to serve themselves more than their clients, and commit themselves to the oath of the court, we'll all be the better for it.

PAMELA ANN RYMER,
LOS ANGELES FEDERAL JUDGE

I'm not an ambulance chaser. I'm usually there before the ambulance.

MELVIN BELLI,
AMERICAN LAWYER

The excesses of today's legal system and those who profess to be its servants in fact amount to a serious problem and are at the root of a festering public disrespect for the law.

SAMUEL JAN BRAKEL, AMERICAN LAWYER

In civilized life, law floats in a sea of ethics. Each is indispensable to civilization. Without law, we should be at the mercy of the least scrupulous; without ethics, law could not exist.

EARL WARREN, SUPREME COURT JUSTICE

Too many lawyers have forgotten that the main purpose of the law profession is to serve the public interest.

PETER BROWN, AMERICAN LAWYER

You just had to take the practical view that a man always lied on his own behalf, and paid his lawyer, who was an expert, a professional liar, to show him new and better ways of lying.

**JAMES GOULD COZZENS,
AMERICAN WRITER**

I don't see why we should not come out roundly and say that one of the functions of a lawyer is to lie for his client; and on rare occasions, as I think I have shown, I believe it is.

**CHARLES P. CURTIS,
AMERICAN LAWYER**

Bar associations are notoriously reluctant to disbar or even suspend a member unless he has murdered a judge downtown at high noon, in the presence of the entire Committee on Ethical Practices.

**SYDNEY J. HARRIS,
BRITISH-AMERICAN WRITER**

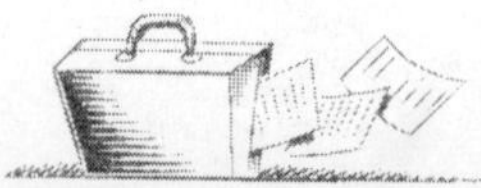

No poet ever interpreted nature as freely
as a lawyer interprets truth.

JEAN GIRAUDOUX,
19TH-CENTURY FRENCH PLAYWRIGHT

What do you get in place of a conscience?
Don't answer, I know: a lawyer.

KIRK DOUGLAS AS DETECTIVE JIM MCLEOD,
IN THE FILM DETECTIVE STORY

The ethical distinction between lying to a jury
and pulling the wool over its eyes is surely a fine one.

PHILLIP E. JOHNSON,
LAW PROFESSOR, UNIVERSITY OF CALIFORNIA

It is difficult to overestimate how responsible
Watergate was for putting the spotlight on legal ethics.

MICHAEL ALAN SCHWARTZ,
AMERICAN JOURNALIST

Just addressed the California State Legislature and helped them pass a bill to form a lawyers' association to regulate their conduct. Personally I don't think you can make a lawyer honest by an act of the Legislature. You've got to work on his conscience. And his lack of conscience is what makes him a lawyer.

WILL ROGERS,
AMERICAN ACTOR AND HUMORIST

Let it be said that we are electing people who . . . will lay aside their own personal shortcomings and have the inner strength to discipline themselves sufficiently that they do not break the law which they themselves are sworn to uphold.

ED BRYANT,
U.S. REPRESENTATIVE FROM TENNESSEE DURING THE CLINTON IMPEACHMENT HEARINGS

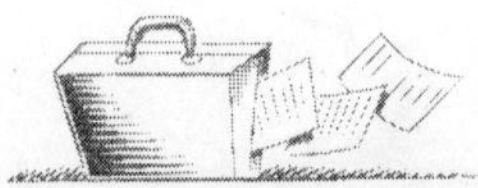

It is safe to assume legal doctrines that claim to be the offspring of logic are either not proud of or not aware of their real parents.

FELIX S. COHEN,
LAWYER AND LEGAL SCHOLAR

Helping people is never more rewarding than when it's in your own self-interest.

GREG GERMANN AS RICHARD FISH,
SENIOR PARTNER IN THE TELEVISION SHOW ALLY MCBEAL

Woe Unto Them

Senator Sam Ervin, of North Carolina, loved to tell the story of a young lawyer who showed up at a revival meeting where he was asked to deliver a prayer. Unprepared, the rookie attorney gave a prayer straight from a veteran lawyer's heart: Stir up much strife amongst thy people, Lord, lest thy servant perish.

Professional Discourtesy

George Ade, a well-known humorist in the early part of the century, had just finished a delightful speech at a banquet and sat down to applause from the crowd.

The master of ceremonies, a well-known lawyer, got to his feet, shoved his hands into his pants pockets, as was his habit, and asked the crowd, "Doesn't it strike anyone as a little unusual that a professional humorist should be funny?"

When the laughter from the audience subsided, Ade stood up and told the crowd, "Doesn't it strike anyone as a little unusual that a lawyer should have his hands in his own pockets?"

"Nod" Guilty

Judge James Darrah of the San Joaquin County (California) Superior Court granted a convicted murderer a new trial in 1989—because the judge confessed that he had fallen asleep during part of a defense witness's testimony.

Judge Darrah found Tab Lee Bennett guilty of murder. But then the judge reconsidered and filed his own affidavit, swearing he had been asleep for 13 minutes of testimony that focused on the description of the scene of the crime. The judge said he couldn't be sure that nodding off didn't have some affect on the verdict.

GOVERNMENT

The more perfect civilization is, the less occasion it has for government, because the more it does to regulate its own affairs, and govern itself. . . . All the great laws of society are laws of nature.

THOMAS PAINE,
18TH-CENTURY BRITISH-BORN AMERICAN POLITICAL PHILOSOPHER AND WRITER

I believe that the law was made for man and not man for the law; that government is the servant of the people and not their master.

JOHN D. ROCKEFELLER, JR.,
AMERICAN OIL MAGNATE AND PHILANTHROPIST

The execution of the laws is more important than the making of them.

THOMAS JEFFERSON,
3RD PRESIDENT OF THE UNITED STATES

The last bastion of protecting everyone's right to freedom is a court of law.

RICHARD ISRAELS, CANADIAN LAWYER

Can any of you seriously say the Bill of Rights could get through Congress today? It wouldn't even get out of committee.

F. LEE BAILEY, AMERICAN LAWYER

Law is not self-executing. Unfortunately, at times its execution rests in the hands of those who are faithless to it. And even when its enforcement is committed to those who revere it, law merely deters some human beings from offending, and punishes other human beings for offending. It does not make men good. This task can be performed only by ethics or religion or morality.

SAMUEL ERVIN, JR., UNITED STATES SENATOR

From Antigone through Martin Luther to Martin Luther King Jr., the issue of liberty has turned on the existence of a higher law than that of the State.

MILTON MAYER,
AMERICAN JOURNALIST

Good laws, if they are not obeyed, do not constitute good government.

ARISTOTLE,
4TH-CENTURY B.C. GREEK PHILOSOPHER

A government of laws, and not of men.

JOHN ADAMS,
2ND PRESIDENT OF THE UNITED STATES

All associations are dangerous to good Government . . . and associations of Lawyers the most dangerous of any next to the Military.

CADWALLADER COLDEN,
17TH-CENTURY IRISH-BORN AMERICAN POLITICIAN

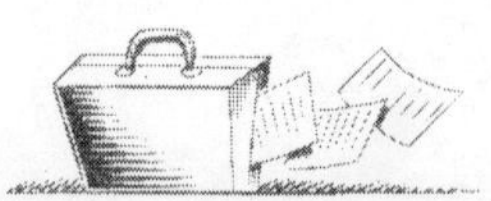

I have come to the conclusion that one useless man is called a disgrace, two men are called a law firm, and three or more become a Congress.

**ATTRIBUTED TO JOHN ADAMS,
2ND PRESIDENT OF THE UNITED STATES,
IN THE PLAY 1776**

Younger people are going to think that Washington is sort of a tragic comedy with everyone sort of doing things that are almost like a bleak carnival that has very little impact on their lives and that is lethal to a democracy.

**MICHAEL BESCHLOSS,
PRESIDENTIAL HISTORIAN**

The crimes of perjury and obstruction of justice, like the crimes of treason and bribery, are quintessentially offenses against our system of government.

**CHARLES J. COOPER,
AMERICAN LAWYER
ON THE IMPEACHMENT OF PRESIDENT CLINTON**

You can't impeach a popular president when you're governing through poll-driven forms of government.

JOAN HOFF,
OHIO UNIVERSITY HISTORIAN
ON THE IMPEACHMENT OF PRESIDENT CLINTON

Proving intent is always difficult. But proving an intent by one person to gratify another is impossible. To give the government the power even to ask the question is to encourage sexual McCarthyism.

ALAN DERSHOWITZ,
AMERICAN LAWYER AND HARVARD LAW PROFESSOR
ON THE IMPEACHMENT OF PRESIDENT CLINTON

The government in which I believe is that which is based on mere moral sanction . . . the real law lives in the kindness of our hearts. If our hearts are empty, no law or political reform can fill them.

LEO TOLSTOY,
19TH-CENTURY RUSSIAN PHILOSOPHER AND AUTHOR

Government is dangerous, so we have to control it. But it's not a necessary evil, it's a necessary good.

GARRY WILLS,
NORTHWESTERN UNIVERSITY HISTORY PROFESSOR

A government big enough to give you everything you want is a government big enough to take from you everything you have.

GERALD R. FORD,
38TH PRESIDENT OF THE UNITED STATES

Poetic Justice

A federal judge in Cincinnati used rhyme and reason when she threw out a lawsuit that challenged Congress authority to set aside a federal holiday for Christmas.

The suit, filed in 1999 by attorney Richard Ganulin, argued that Congress long ago violated the concept of church-state separation when Christmas became a national holiday.

In her ruling, U.S. District Judge Susan J. Dlott wrote:

We are all better for Santa, the Easter Bunny too,
And maybe the Great Pumpkin, to name just a few.
An extra day off is hardly high treason;
It may be spent as you wish, regardless of reason.
One is never jailed, for not having a tree,
For not going to church, for not spreading glee!
The court will uphold, seemingly contradictory causes,
Decreeing 'The Establishment' and 'Santa' both
worthwhile claus(es).

Open Season on Lawyers

Before adjourning its session in 1989, the Virginia legislature jokingly considered a bill establishing a new sport—hunting for attorneys!

The bill was referred to the state game board for a determination of whether lawyers should be deemed a nuisance species. Under the bill, using cash as bait and shouting "whiplash" and "ambulance" to trap lawyers would be strictly prohibited.

The bill for an open season on lawyers failed to pass.

LAW SCHOOL

Doctors and lawyers must go to school for years and years, often with little sleep and with great sacrifice to their first wives.

ROY BLOUNT, JR.,
AMERICAN WRITER

Be prepared, be sharp, be careful, and use the King's English well. And you can forget all the [other rules] unless you remember one more: Get paid.

ROBERT N. C. NIX,
UNITED STATES CONGRESSMAN,
GIVING ADVICE TO YOUNG LAWYERS AT HIS SON'S GRADUATION FROM LAW SCHOOL

Law school taught me one thing: how to take two situations that are exactly the same and show how they are different.

HART POMERANTZ,
AMERICAN LAWYER

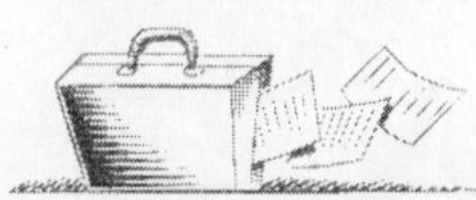

Law students are trained in the case method, and, to the lawyer, everything in life looks like a case. His first thought in the morning is how to handle the case of the ringing alarm clock.

EDWARD B. PACKARD, JR., AMERICAN LAWYER

We must begin to train lawyers the minute they walk into law school to tell the truth. They must immediately begin to learn the business of representing people. They must be assigned cases the first day.

GERRY SPENCE, AMERICAN LAWYER

Law school has been described as a place for the accumulation of learning. First-year students bring some in; third-year students take none away. Hence it accumulates.

DANIEL R. WHITE, AMERICAN WRITER

Good law schools teach you to think like lawyers. But the top law schools teach young people to think; just to think. And that makes a potentially great lawyer.

NORM SHERMAN,
AMERICAN LAWYER

Law school attempts to profoundly alter the way you think. A challenging but sometimes wrenching experience.

RAY BROWN,
AMERICAN LAWYER

If the weakness of the apprentice system was to produce advocates without scholarship, the weakness of the law school system is to turn out scholars with no skill at advocacy.

ROBERT H. JACKSON,
SUPREME COURT JUSTICE

The bar exam is a multi-part torture designed
by people whose sole purpose in life is to
stem the tide of incoming attorneys.

ANONYMOUS ATTORNEY,
ON-LINE MAGAZINE TILT

There is no better way to exercise the imagination than
the study of the law. No artist ever interpreted nature
as freely as a lawyer interprets the truth.

JEAN GIRAUDOUX,
19TH-CENTURY FRENCH PLAYWRIGHT

If law school is so hard to get through,
how come there are so many lawyers?

CALVIN TRILLIN,
AMERICAN WRITER

Leave it to Beaver

As a young deputy district attorney in Kern County, California, in 1973, H. Dennis Beaver was trying a consumer fraud case before Judge Walter Conley. But the judge rapidly grew exasperated with the rookie lawyer's line of questioning.

"If you keep on asking these idiotic questions, I am going to send you some place where you have never been," the judge warned Beaver.

"You mean jail, your honor?" Beaver asked.

"No," replied the judge. "Law school!"

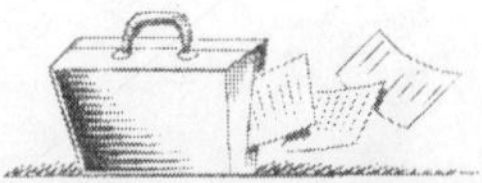

And What About the Benefits?

When Judge Richard Neely of Charleston, West Virginia, was seeking new law clerks in 1991, he ran the following ad in the *University of Virginia Law Weekly*:

"West Virginia's infamous once and future Justice Richard Neely, America's laziest and dumbest judge, seeks a bright person to keep him from looking stupid. Preference will be given to U. Va. law students who studied interesting but useless subjects at snobby schools. If you are dead drunk and miss the interviews, send letters."

OBEYING THE LAW

The mass of the people have nothing to do with the laws but to obey them.

SAMUEL HORSLEY, 18TH-CENTURY ENGLISH BISHOP

One has not only a legal but a moral responsibility to obey just laws. Conversely, one has a moral responsibility to disobey unjust laws.

DR. MARTIN LUTHER KING, JR., AMERICAN CLERGYMAN AND CIVIL RIGHTS LEADER

No man in this country is so high that he is above the law. No officer of the law may set that law at defiance with impunity. All the officers of the government, from the highest to the lowest, are creatures of the law, and are bound to obey it.

SAMUEL F. MILLER, 19TH-CENTURY AMERICAN JUDGE

In a democracy only those laws which have their bases in folkways or the approval of strong groups have a chance of being enforced.

ABRAHAM MYERSON,
RUSSIAN-AMERICAN NEUROPSYCHIATRIST

There's a lot of law at the end of a nightstick.

GROVER A. WHALEN,
NEW YORK CITY POLICE COMMISSIONER

Anyone who takes it upon himself, on his private authority, to break a bad law, thereby authorizes everyone else to break the good ones.

DENIS DIDEROT,
18TH-CENTURY FRENCH ENCYCLOPEDIST

Good men must not obey the laws too well.

RALPH WALDO EMERSON,
19TH-CENTURY AMERICAN POET AND WRITER

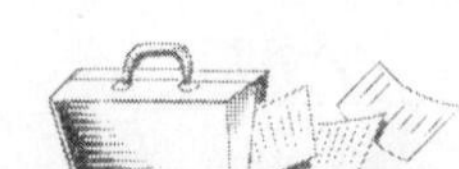

Laws were made to be broken.

CHRISTOPHER NORTH,
18TH-CENTURY SCOTTISH WRITER

The best use of good laws is to teach men to trample bad laws under their feet.

WENDELL PHILLIPS,
19TH-CENTURY AMERICAN ORATOR AND REFORMER

There are not enough jails, not enough policemen, not enough courts to enforce a law not supported by the people.

HUBERT HUMPHREY,
38TH VICE PRESIDENT OF THE UNITED STATES

To make laws that man cannot, and will not obey, serves to bring all law into contempt.

ELIZABETH CADY STANTON,
19TH-CENTURY AMERICAN SUFFRAGIST

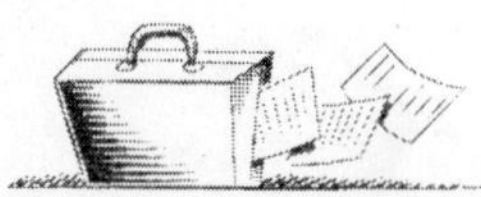

There is no man so good, who, were he to submit all his thoughts and action to the laws, would not deserve hanging ten times in his life.

MICHEL DE MONTAIGNE,
16TH-CENTURY FRENCH WRITER

It ain't no sin if you crack a few laws now and then, just so long as you don't break any.

MAE WEST AS PEACHES O'DAY,
IN THE FILM EVERY DAY'S A HOLIDAY

Late every night in Connecticut, lights go out in the cities and towns, and citizens by tens of thousands proceed zestfully to break the law. Of course, there is always a witness to the crime—but as though to make the law completely unenforceable, Connecticut forbids spouses from testifying against one another.

TIME MAGAZINE,
ON THE CONNECTICUT LAW AGAINST
CONTRACEPTIVES, 1961

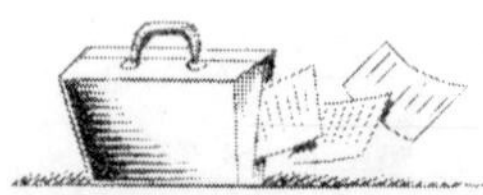

No man is above the law and no man is below it; nor do we ask any man's permission when we ask him to obey it.

THEODORE ROOSEVELT,
26TH PRESIDENT OF THE UNITED STATES

The notorious lawlessness of the Commander has passed into a proverb, familiar to man-of-war's men: The law was not made for the Captain!

HERMAN MELVILLE,
19TH-CENTURY AMERICAN WRITER

Whether ours shall continue to be a government of laws and not of men is now for Congress and ultimately the American people to decide.

ARCHIBALD COX,
WATERGATE PROSECUTOR,
AFTER BEING DISMISSED BY PRESIDENT RICHARD NIXON BECAUSE HE REFUSED TO DROP HIS LAWSUIT TO OBTAIN WATERGATE-RELATED WHITE HOUSE TAPES

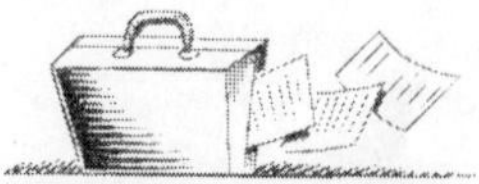

When the President does it, that means it is not illegal.

RICHARD NIXON,
37TH PRESIDENT OF THE UNITED STATES

If Nixon is not forced to turn over tapes of his conversations with the ring of men who were conversing on their violations of the law, then liberty will soon be dead in this nation.

WILLIAM O. DOUGLAS,
SUPREME COURT JUSTICE

The illegal we do immediately. The unconstitutional takes a little longer.

HENRY KISSINGER,
NATIONAL SECURITY ADVISOR
AND SECRETARY OF STATE IN THE NIXON ADMINISTRATION

A man's respect for law and order exists in precise relationship to the size of his paycheck.

ADAM CLAYTON POWELL, JR.,
AMERICAN CLERGYMAN AND UNITED STATES CONGRESSMAN

Laws made by common consent must not be trampled on by individuals.

GEORGE WASHINGTON,
1ST PRESIDENT OF THE UNITED STATES

An individual who breaks a law that his conscience tells him is unjust, and who willingly accepts the penalty of imprisonment in order to arouse the conscience of the community over its injustice, is in reality expressing the highest respect for law.

DR. MARTIN LUTHER KING, JR.,
AMERICAN CLERGYMAN AND CIVIL RIGHTS LEADER

The President again took an oath to tell the truth, the whole truth, and nothing but the truth. The evidence demonstrates that the president failed to adhere to that oath and thus to his presidential oath to faithfully execute the laws.

KENNETH STARR,
SPECIAL PROSECUTOR FOR THE WHITEWATER INVESTIGATION

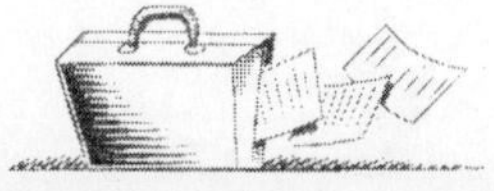

He who lives in solitude may make his own laws.

PUBLILIUS SYRUS,
1ST-CENTURY B.C. ROMAN WRITER

If he who breaks the law is not punished,
he who obeys it is cheated.

DR. THOMAS SZASZ,
PROFESSOR, SYRACUSE UNIVERSITY

Rigid laws are brittle, not strong, and easily broken.

THOMAS A. WARTOWSKI,
AMERICAN LAWYER

Perjury primarily and directly injures the body politic,
for it subverts the judicial process and this strikes
at the heart of the rule of law itself.

CHARLES J. COOPER,
AMERICAN LAWYER

What About the Tooth Fairy?

The U.S. District Court for the Southern District in Ohio didn't believe the testimony of an alleged drug dealer.

In a 1981 ruling the court wrote, "Defendant and his common-law wife . . . had a combined drug habit of between $60 and $120 per day. This court, not believing in Santa Claus and having severe reservations about the existence of the Easter Bunny, must conclude that one does not support a wife and three children and a drug habit of some $60 to $120 a day on a $267 per month welfare check."

Fast Introduction

One day in 1993, Atlanta attorney Dennis Scheib stopped by the prosecutor's office on his way to court to represent a new client in a criminal case. Just outside the office, the lawyer saw two officers chasing a man down the hall, so Scheib joined in to help. The trio

managed to catch the man who was quickly subdued and handcuffed. Only then did Scheib learn the man's identity—he was the new client that the lawyer was going to represent.

Winner Take All

Attorney Arlo Sommervold of Sioux Falls, South Dakota, was representing a defendant charged with stealing hogs during a 1991 trial.

After Sommervold put on a spirited defense, the jury deliberated for a short while and then returned with its verdict. The jury foreman announced, "We the jury acquit the defendant."

Sommervold turned to shake hands with his client, who then asked, "Does this mean I can keep the hogs?"

JUSTICE

Wrong must not win by technicalities.

AESCHYLUS,
6TH-CENTURY B.C. GREEK DRAMATIST

When it comes to justice, I take no prisoners
and I don't believe in compromising.

MARY FRANCES BERRY,
AMERICAN LEGAL SCHOLAR AND
CIVIL RIGHTS ACTIVIST

But let judgment run down as waters,
and righteousness as a mighty stream.

AMOS, 5:24

Get out of the way of Justice. She is blind.

STANISLAW LEC,
CZECH WRITER

Though justice moves slowly, it seldom fails to overtake the wicked.

HORACE,
1ST-CENTURY B.C. ROMAN POET AND SATIRIST

The wheels of justice . . . they're square wheels.

BARBARA CORCORAN,
AMERICAN WRITER

There is no such thing as justice—in or out of court.

CLARENCE DARROW,
AMERICAN LAWYER AND WRITER

Justice is the end of government.

DANIEL DEFOE,
17TH-CENTURY ENGLISH WRITER

Sir, I say that justice is truth in action.

BENJAMIN DISRAELI,
19TH-CENTURY BRITISH PRIME MINISTER

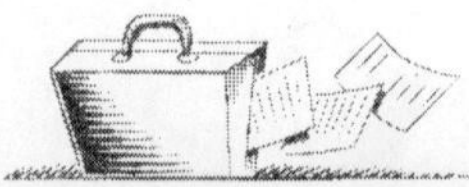

I tell ye Hogan's right when he says: "Justice is blind." Blind she is, an' deef an' dumb an' has a wooden leg!

MR. DOOLEY [FINLEY PETER DUNNE], AMERICAN HUMORIST

If we are to keep our democracy, there must be one commandment: Thou shalt not ration justice.

LEARNED HAND, U.S. COURT OF APPEALS JUDGE

Justice, n. A commodity which in a more or less adulterated condition the State sells to the citizen as a reward for his allegiance, taxes, and personal service.

AMBROSE BIERCE, AMERICAN WRITER

The primary duty of a lawyer engaged in public prosecution is not to convict, but to see that justice is done.

CANONS OF PROFESSIONAL ETHICS, CANON 5

Justice is incidental to law and order.

**J. EDGAR HOOVER,
DIRECTOR, FBI**

Justice should remove the bandage from her eyes long enough to distinguish between the vicious and the unfortunate.

**ROBERT G. INGERSOLL,
19TH-CENTURY AMERICAN LAWYER**

Justice is the right of the weaker.

**JOSEPH JOUBERT,
18TH-CENTURY FRENCH WRITER AND MORALIST**

As soon as I set myself up as the judge and jury, I might as well be the executioner.

**RICHARD ISRAELS,
CANADIAN LAWYER**

White folks don't want peace; they want quiet. The price you pay for peace is justice. Until there is justice, there will be no peace and quiet.

JESSE JACKSON,
AMERICAN CLERGYMAN AND
CIVIL RIGHTS LEADER

A right is not what someone gives you; it's what no one can take from you.

RAMSEY CLARK,
U.S. ATTORNEY GENERAL

Justice delayed is democracy denied.

ROBERT F. KENNEDY,
U.S. ATTORNEY GENERAL

I have a saying—there's no justice in the law.

ELLEN MORPHONIOS,
AMERICAN JUDGE ALSO KNOWN AS
"MAXIMUM MORPHONIOS"

This court will not deny the equal protection of the law to the unwashed, unshod, unkempt, and uninhibited.

HERMAN WEINKRANTZ,
AMERICAN JUDGE

There is no authority without justice.

NAPOLEON I,
EMPEROR OF FRANCE

Justice and judgment lie often a world apart.

EMMELINE PANKHURST,
ENGLISH SUFFRAGIST

The fundamentals of justice are that no one shall suffer wrong, and that the public good be served.

CICERO,
2ND-CENTURY B.C. ROMAN
STATESMAN, ORATOR, AND WRITER

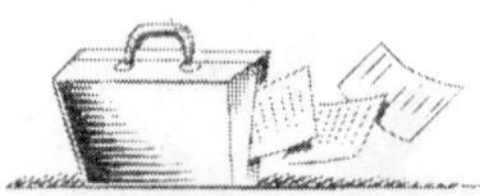

Fairness is what justice really is.

POTTER STEWART,
SUPREME COURT JUSTICE

Judging from the main portions of
the history of the world so far,
justice is always in jeopardy.

WALT WHITMAN,
19TH-CENTURY AMERICAN POET

Unless justice be done to others
it will not be done to us.

WOODROW WILSON,
28TH PRESIDENT OF THE UNITED STATES

Justice, though she's painted blind
Is to the weaker side inclined.

SAMUEL BUTLER,
17TH-CENTURY ENGLISH SATIRICAL POET

Justice is like a train that's nearly always late.

YEVGENY YEVTUSHENKO,
RUSSIAN POET

The achievement of justice is an endless process.

JOHN F. KENNEDY,
35TH PRESIDENT OF THE UNITED STATES

Justice is lame as well as blind.

THOMAS OTWAY,
17TH-CENTURY ENGLISH DRAMATIST

Rather suffer an injustice than commit one.

YIDDISH PROVERB

Every virtue is included in the idea of justice,
and every just man is good.

THEOGNIS,
6TH-CENTURY B.C. GREEK POET

Let justice be done, though the world perish.

MOTTO OF FERDINAND I,
HOLY ROMAN EMPEROR

Justice may wink a while, but see at last.

THOMAS MIDDLETON,
16TH-CENTURY ENGLISH DRAMATIST

You may not find justice in the courtroom,
but you usually get what you deserve.

DAVID SPICER,
AMERICAN LAWYER

One hour of justice is worth a hundred of prayer.

ARAB PROVERB

Justice is always violent to the party offending,
for every man is innocent in his own eyes.

DANIEL DEFOE,
17TH-CENTURY ENGLISH WRITER

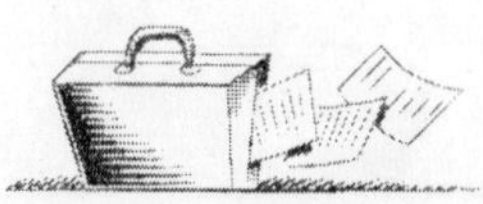

Justice is my being allowed to do whatever I like.
Injustice is whatever prevents my doing so.

SAMUEL BUTLER,
19TH-CENTURY ENGLISH JOURNALIST AND WRITER

Justice is the great standing policy of civil society.

EDMUND BURKE,
18TH-CENTURY ENGLISH STATESMAN AND ORATOR

Absolute freedom mocks at justice.
Absolute justice denies freedom.

ALBERT CAMUS,
FRENCH WRITER

Justice? You get justice in the next world,
in this world you have the law.

WILLIAM GADDIS,
WRITER

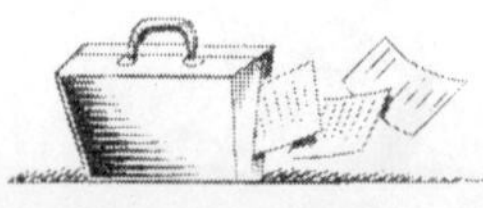

Whereas in Greek the idea of justice was akin to harmony, in Hebrew it is akin to holiness.

JOSEPH H. HERTZ,
BRITISH-BORN HUNGARIAN RABBI

Justice is the earnest and constant will to render to every man his due. The precepts of the law are these: to live honorably, to injure no other man, to render to every man his due.

JUSTINIAN I,
EMPEROR OF BYZANTINE

The love of justice is simply, in the majority of men, the fear of suffering injustice.

FRANÇOIS DE LA ROCHEFOUCAULD,
17TH-CENTURY FRENCH WRITER

Justice is the only thing that allowed the human race to stop living as animals and to start living as human beings.

FRANK W. WILSON,
AMERICAN JUDGE

If we do not maintain Justice, Justice will not maintain us.

FRANCIS BACON,
ENGLISH PHILOSOPHER AND WRITER

The greatest dangers to liberty lurk in insidious encroachment by men of zeal, well-meaning but without understanding.

LOUIS D. BRANDEIS,
SUPREME COURT JUSTICE

Justice seems to drown in a sea of "technicalities" . . . in order to have equal justice there must be some rules which are applied evenly . . . to all regardless of power, gender, lifestyle, race, etc.

RAY BROWN,
AMERICAN LAWYER

Whenever a separation is made between liberty and justice, neither, in my opinion, is safe.

EDMUND BURKE,
BRITISH POLITICAL PHILOSOPHER AND STATESMAN

They [lawyers] talk about law—why, gentlemen, it's not law we want, but justice.

JOHN DUDLEY,
18TH-CENTURY JUDGE

[The law] is a very imperfect mechanism. If you press exactly the right buttons and are also lucky, justice may show up in the answer.

RAYMOND CHANDLER,
AMERICAN WRITER

Extremism in the defense of liberty is no vice. And moderation in the pursuit of justice is no virtue.

BARRY GOLDWATER,
AMERICAN STATESMAN

I think that there are certain crimes which the law cannot touch, and which therefore, to some extent, justify private revenge.

SHERLOCK HOLMES,
FICTIONAL DETECTIVE CREATED BY
BRITISH WRITER SIR ARTHUR CONAN DOYLE

The United States wins its point when justice is done for its citizens in the courts.

INSCRIPTION INSIDE THE JUSTICE DEPARTMENT BUILDING

Justice is a by-product of winning.

SAM WATERSTON AS JACK MCCOY,
DISTRICT ATTORNEY IN THE TELEVISION SHOW LAW AND ORDER

Nothing is to be preferred before justice.

SOCRATES,
4TH-CENTURY B.C. GREEK PHILOSOPHER

As Mankind becomes more liberal, they will be more apt to allow that all those who conduct themselves as worthy members of the community are equally entitled to the protections of civil government. I hope ever to see America among the foremost nations of justice and liberality.

GEORGE WASHINGTON,
1ST PRESIDENT OF THE UNITED STATES

When there are too many policemen, there can be no liberty; When there are too many soldiers, there can be no peace; When there are too many lawyers, there can be no justice.

LIN YUTANG,
CHINESE WRITER

Habeas corpus isn't just a quaint Latin phrase. It was the key to my freedom.

RUBIN "HURRICANE" CARTER,
AMERICAN BOXER FREED AFTER 19 YEARS IN PRISON FOR A CRIME HE DIDN'T COMMIT

It Takes Two

Judge William C. Miller of Montgomery County, Maryland, was hearing a 1990 case in which the defendant had skipped his court date.

Miller announced he was going to issue a bench warrant to have the defendant picked up.

"You can't do that," said the public defender. "The man is a schizophrenic."

"In that case," replied the judge, "I'll issue two."

Seeking Body and Soul

Lawyer Amy Jackson of the Legal Aid Society of Salt Lake City, Utah, was discussing a family law case with her paralegal one day in 1993. The client had filled out an application with the legal aid society that stated she wanted "soul" custody.

Seeing the error, the paralegal remarked, "I'm not sure we can get jurisdiction."

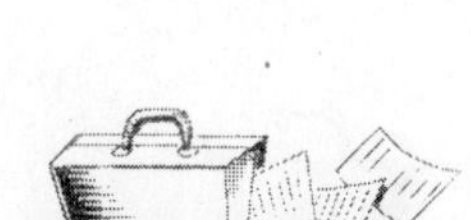

House Calls

Doctors may not make house calls anymore, but Memphis Criminal Court Judge Joe B. Brown has. The former criminal defense attorney has on several occasions accepted guilty pleas from burglars and then attached an unusual condition. Their victims get to drop by the thieves' houses and take something from them!

In 1991, Brown's sentence was carried out by business executive Lionel Winston, whose housekeeper had stolen from him. Accompanied by Judge Brown and a sheriff's deputy, Winston paid two unannounced visits to the ex-housekeeper's house and claimed two coats that he later gave away.

"I asked [the convict] how it felt to lose a possession and he said, 'Not so good,'" Winston recalled. "I said, 'Now you know how it felt.'"

A Wife Sentence

A judge known for his unusual sentences made marriage a mandatory condition in a defendant's plea bargain.

When Kevin Musser was convicted of assaulting his live-in girlfriend in 1992, Citrus County (Florida) Judge Gary Graham told him, "You have a choice. Marry the mother of your children and get a year's probation or never see her again and get a year in jail."

Musser chose to be sentenced to marriage rather than the hoosegow.

And Toto Too?

Referring to a scene from the classic movie *The Wizard of Oz* nearly got a defense attorney cited for contempt.

During sentencing in a criminal trial in Dayton (Ohio) Municipal Court in 1989, Judge Michael Merz read aloud from the defendant's rap sheet, "Convicted of manslaughter in 1957 in Kansas." Judge Merz then asked defense counsel George E. Zimmerman, "Do you have any suggestions as to how we can get your client back to Kansas?"

Replied the quick-witted attorney, "How about if I have him click his heels together three times?" Realizing his wit might get him into trouble, Zimmerman added, "Oh, I'm sorry, your honor."

"That's too funny to be contemptuous, counselor," said Judge Merz. "Perhaps the workhouse will better suit him for the next six months."

INJUSTICE

When one has been threatened
with a great injustice,
one accepts a smaller as a favor.

JANE WELSH CARLYLE,
19TH-CENTURY SCOTTISH POET

"No, no!" said the Queen.
"Sentence first—verdict afterwards."

FROM LEWIS CARROLL'S
ALICE'S ADVENTURES IN WONDERLAND

We have accumulated a wealth of historical
experience which confirms our belief that
the scales of American justice are out of balance.

ANGELA YVONNE DAVIS,
AMERICAN CIVIL RIGHTS ACTIVIST AND EDUCATOR

Extreme justice is extreme injustice.

CICERO,
1ST-CENTURY B.C. ROMAN STATESMAN,
ORATOR, AND WRITER

National injustice is the surest road
to national downfall.

WILLIAM EVARTS,
19TH-CENTURY AMERICAN LAWYER

Justice delayed is justice denied.

WILLIAM E. GLADSTONE,
19TH-CENTURY BRITISH STATESMAN

Since when do you have to agree with people
to defend them from injustice?

LILLIAN HELLMAN,
AMERICAN DRAMATIST

Injustice anywhere is a threat to justice everywhere.

DR. MARTIN LUTHER KING, JR.,
AMERICAN CLERGYMAN AND CIVIL RIGHTS LEADER

Injustice is relatively easy to bear;
what stings is justice.

H. L. MENCKEN,
AMERICAN JOURNALIST

A kingdom founded on injustice never lasts.

SENECA,
1ST-CENTURY ROMAN STATESMAN
AND PHILOSOPHER

One had better die fighting against injustice
than die like a dog or a rat in a trap.

IDA B. WELLS,
AMERICAN JOURNALIST

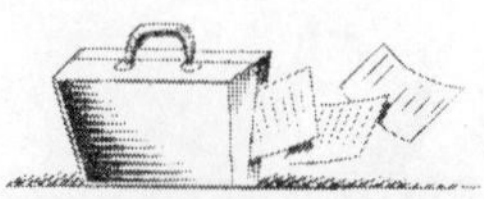

It would have cost me more trouble to escape from injustice, than it does to submit to it.

JEANNE-MARIE ROLAND,
18TH-CENTURY FRENCH REVOLUTIONARY

The court is most merciful when the accused is most rich.

HEBREW PROVERB

Whenever men take the law into their own hands, the loser is the law. And when the law loses, freedom languishes.

ROBERT F. KENNEDY,
U.S. ATTORNEY GENERAL

In our courts, when it's a white man's word against a black man's, the white man always wins. They're ugly, but those are the facts of life.

HARPER LEE,
AMERICAN WRITER

That which is not just is not law.

WILLIAM LLOYD GARRISON,
AMERICAN ABOLITIONIST

If it is of such a nature that it requires you to be the agent of injustice to another, then, I say, break the law. Let your life be a counter-friction to stop the machine [government].

HENRY DAVID THOREAU,
AMERICAN WRITER

Split Personality

In 1995, an attorney representing himself in a suit for recovery of his own fees had his case dismissed because he failed to appear for a hearing in the Los Angeles Municipal Court. He subsequently filed a motion requesting the suit be reinstated because, he said, it wouldn't be fair to penalize the client for the mistake of his attorney.

The defendants filed their opposition to the motion. Alluding to the famous woman with multiple personalities, the defendants dubbed his argument (which he lost) "the Sybil defense."

You've Got Him!

During a 1991 civil case in Cook County (Illinois) Circuit Court, an attorney was doing a particularly skillful job of cross-examining a witness.

Question by question, he laid a trap that seemed inescapable. When he asked the final question, the judge could stand it no longer. Before the witness could answer, the judge yelled, "You've got him! You've got him!"

The case settled during a short recess.

JUSTICE
JUSTICE

THE WHEELS OF JUSTICE

LITIGATION

In the strange heat all litigation brings to bear on things, the very process of litigation fosters the most profound misunderstandings in the world.

RENATA ADLER,
ITALIAN-BORN AMERICAN WRITER,
FILM CRITIC, AND PHILOSOPHER

As a people we must somehow get over the notion that the solution to every problem is a lawsuit.

ERNEST CONINE,
AMERICAN JOURNALIST

Criticizing lawyers for lawsuits is like criticizing linebackers for knocking people down.

DALE DAUTEN,
NEWSPAPER COLUMNIST

More lawsuits may not be good for large corporations,but they are good for justice and society, especially if brought by the powerless against the powerful.

ALAN DERSHOWITZ,
LAWYER AND HARVARD LAW PROFESSOR

The courtrooms of America all too often have Piper Cub advocates trying to handle the controls of Boeing 747 litigation.

WARREN BURGER,
SUPREME COURT JUSTICE

To seek the redress of grievances by going to law is like sheep running for shelter to a bramble bush.

LEWIS W. DILLWYN,
18TH-CENTURY ENGLISH NATURALIST

A lean compromise is better than a fat lawsuit.

ENGLISH PROVERB

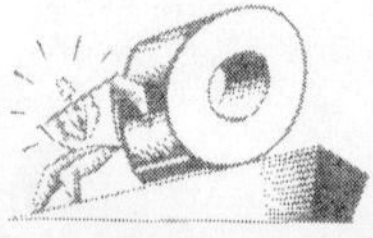

A lawsuit is a fruit tree planted in a lawyer's garden.

ITALIAN PROVERB

The American liability lawsuit mess is the corporate version of the weather—everyone talks about it, but nothing ever happens.

THE CORPORATE BOARD

We lawyers know well, and may cite high authority for it if required, that life would be intolerable if every man insisted on his legal rights to the full.

**FREDERICK POLLOCK,
ENGLISH JUDGE**

Never stir up litigation. A worse man can scarcely be found than one who does this.

**ABRAHAM LINCOLN,
16TH PRESIDENT OF THE UNITED STATES**

It is becoming increasingly clear that litigation is threatening our national economic viability. Sheer numbers tell the story.

J. DANFORTH QUAYLE,
44TH VICE PRESIDENT OF THE UNITED STATES

A simple principle supports the medical litigation industry. Sue often enough, and eventually a sympathetic jury will return an outlandish verdict.

LINDA SEEBACH,
AMERICAN JOURNALIST

The issues can be analyzed in pages less than fifty
If plaintiffs could with thought and words
endeavor to be thrifty.

ASHER RUBIN,
CALIFORNIA DEPUTY ATTORNEY GENERAL,
REPLYING IN RHYME TO THE LAWYERS
FOR THE OPPOSITION WHO SUBMITTED
THEIR SECOND REQUEST TO FILE A BRIEF THAT
EXCEEDED THE COURT'S 50-PAGE LIMIT

Litigation should be a last resort, not a knee-jerk reflex.

IRVING S. SHAPIRO,
AMERICAN INDUSTRIALIST

We have too many lawyers chasing too many dollars
through too many endless lawsuits,
and it is time to do something about it.

CASPAR W. WEINBERGER,
PUBLISHER OF FORBES

Litigation takes the place of sex at middle age.

GORE VIDAL,
AMERICAN WRITER

Four out of five potential litigants will settle their disputes the first day they come together, if you will put the idea of arbitration into their heads.

MOSES HENRY GROSSMAN,
AMERICAN JUDGE

A court is a place where what was confused before becomes more unsettled than ever.

HENRY WALDORF FRANCIS

Discourage litigation. Persuade your neighbors to compromise whenever you can . . . As a peace-maker, the lawyer has a superior opportunity of being a good man. There will still be business enough.

ABRAHAM LINCOLN,
16TH PRESIDENT OF THE UNITED STATES

Most legal cases are swimming in human interest—like bacteria in a petri dish.

CAMERON STRACHER,
AMERICAN LAWYER

Litigation is a machine which you go into
as a pig and come out as a sausage.

AMBROSE BIERCE,
AMERICAN WRITER

It's better to enter the mouth of a tiger
than a court of law.

CHINESE PROVERB

Imagine the appeals, dissents and remandments, if
lawyers had written the Ten Commandments.

HARRY BENDER

I was never ruined but twice—once when I lost
a lawsuit, and once when I gained one.

VOLTAIRE,
18TH CENTURY FRENCH WRITER

That's Not What I Pictured

Pennsylvania lawyer James Sposito sued the publisher of a phone book in 1989 for defamation of character and breach of contract.

Sposito paid for an ad in the phone book promoting his specialty—personal injury cases. The ad was supposed to be illustrated with a picture of two vehicles crashing. Unfortunately, the vehicles pictured next to his name in the ad were ambulances.

Suit Yourself

A man sued himself for trying to raid his own trust fund. Oreste Lodi filed suit against himself in the Shasta County (California) Superior Court. When the judged threw it out, Lodi appealed to the Third Appellate District in 1985 which affirmed the lower court's ruling. "In the arena of pleadings, the one at issue here is a slam-dunk frivolous complaint," said the court.

In making its ruling, the court added, "this result cannot be unfair to Mr. Lodi. Although it is true that,

as plaintiff and appellant, he loses, it is equally true that, as defendant and respondent, he wins! It is hard to imagine a more even handed application of justice. Truly, it would appear that Oreste Lodi is that rare litigant who is assured of both victory and defeat regardless of which side triumphs."

Litigating Circumstances

The county court in Fairfax, Virginia, had been chosen to test a two-year, small-claims program allowing citizens to file a civil lawsuit for up to $1,000. To keep it a true "people's court," all plaintiffs and defendants represented themselves. Cases were decided rapidly because there weren't many legal technicalities to debate. In the third week, however, two opposing litigants happened to be attorneys.

After the proceedings had dragged on for hours, the judge called a recess and stormed into the court clerk's office. "All right," he growled, "who let those lawyers in disguised as real people?"

THE TRIAL

Trial, n.: A formal inquiry designed to prove and put upon record the blameless characters of judges, advocates and jurors.

AMBROSE BIERCE,
AMERICAN WRITER

The trial of a case (is) a three-legged stool—a judge and two advocates.

WARREN BURGER,
SUPREME COURT JUSTICE

I love judges, and I love courts. They are my ideals, that typify on earth what we shall meet hereafter in heaven under a just God.

WILLIAM HOWARD TAFT,
27TH PRESIDENT OF THE UNITED STATES

The penalty for laughing in the courtroom is
six months in jail: if it were not for this penalty,
the jury would never hear the evidence.

H. L. MENCKEN,
AMERICAN JOURNALIST

This is a court of law, young man,
not a court of justice.

OLIVER WENDELL HOLMES, JR.,
SUPREME COURT JUSTICE

This is not a court of love, of compassion,
but a court of law.

DANIEL COBURN,
AMERICAN LAWYER

All sides in a trial want to hide
at least some of the truth.

ALAN DERSHOWITZ,
LAWYER AND HARVARD LAW PROFESSOR

Laws are a dead letter without courts to expound and define their true meaning and operation.

ALEXANDER HAMILTON,
AMERICAN STATESMAN

It's the greatest murder trial of the century—about every two years another one of 'em comes along.

FRANCES NOYES HART,
AMERICAN WRITER

The criminal trial today is . . . a kind of show-jumping contest in which the rider for the prosecution must clear every obstacle to succeed.

ROBERT MARK,
BRITISH POLICE COMMISSIONER

Judge: Are you trying to show contempt for the court?
Flower Belle Lee: No, I'm doing my best to hide it.

W. C. FIELDS AND MAE WEST,
IN THE FILM MY LITTLE CHICKADEE

Starting off [a trial] with a completely open mind is a terribly dangerous thing to do.

RT. HON. SIR MELFORD STEVENSON, BRITISH JUDGE

Trying a case the second time is like eating yesterday morning's oatmeal.

LLOYD PAUL STRYKER, AMERICAN LAWYER

Trials are the most entertaining of all American spectacles, always better than the theater, and except for a few special cases, much more thrilling than movies.

JOHN WATERS, AMERICAN FILMMAKER

Can our courts remain completely independent if they become stages for a continuing television series? I think not. . . . Hear—but we don't need to see.

EUGENE PAVALON,
PRESIDENT, AMERICAN TRIAL LAWYERS ASSOCIATION,
ARGUING AGAINST ALLOWING CAMERAS IN COURTROOMS

I'm worried about so much filth and indecent material coming in through the airwaves and through these trials into people's homes. I think the American people have a right to be protected against some of these excesses. While people have a right to a fair trial, I think the American people have an overriding right to let those matters be decided behind closed doors.

GEORGE BUSH,
41ST PRESIDENT OF THE UNITED STATES,
REFERRING TO THE WILLIAM KENNEDY SMITH RAPE TRIAL

Both consciously and unconsciously, all of the actors in a trial from complaining witnesses and arresting officers through jurors and appeals court judges are frequently and profoundly influenced by race and class.

RAY BROWN,
AMERICAN LAWYER

There is no law in this land about being a little rude in a deposition.

BILL GATES,
CEO OF MICROSOFT

In Other Words

Circuit Judge Ralph Anderson, of South Carolina, showed his love for words was as great as his love for law. In a ruling that left lawyers scrambling for their dictionaries, he wrote in part:

"The evidentiary record consisting of a four (4) day trial is gargantuan, elephantine, and Brobdingnagian. . . . It would be hebetudinous and obtuse to fail to be cognizant of the adverse consequences of a ruling in this case. However, a decision by the court should not be infected with pusillanimity and timidity. The karma of this case must not be aleatory or adventitious, but a pellucid and transpicuous analysis of the law and facts. . . . With certitude and intrepidity and hopefully, with some degree of sagacity, sapience, and perspicaciousness, this court disposes of the relevant and germane issues.

"Autochthonously, this court bifurcates the issues for decisional purposes. The primigenial issue is whether a new trial should be granted. The court comes to this infrangible, ineluctable, and adamantine conclusion that defendant's motion for a new trial absolutely must be denied. The French phrase 'pas du tout' is applied in rejecting the defendant's argument. . . . I find defendant's degree of culpability to be magnitudinous and megatherine."

The Name Game

When Jana K. Miller was a new assistant district attorney working on a case, she ran across the unusual name of Fnu Lnu.

"I tried to check Mr. Lnu on the computer for any previous record, and was presented with pages and pages of Fnu Lnus to pick from," she recalled. "I told my chief prosecutor that I couldn't figure out which Fnu Lnu to pursue because there were too many to check. Was I embarrassed when she told me that Fnu Lnu meant 'First name unknown; Last name unknown.'"

THE VERDICT

It's like seeing your mother-in-law
drive over a cliff in your new Cadillac.

**DON BARRETT,
AMERICAN LAWYER,
DESCRIBING HIS REACTION WHEN JURORS FOUND FOR
HIS CLIENT BUT AWARDED NO DAMAGES BECAUSE
THEY SAID BOTH PARTIES WERE AT FAULT**

The message of the jury sent out basically is that
if you don't believe or agree with a verdict,
it is OK to go out into the streets, to choose certain
fellow human beings, throw rocks at their cars,
beat them up, and take their property.

**ANONYMOUS ALTERNATE JUROR,
AFTER TWO MEN WERE ACQUITTED OF THE
MOST SERIOUS CHARGES IN THE BEATING OF
TRUCK DRIVER REGINALD DENNY DURING
THE 1992 LOS ANGELES RIOTS**

I think that society is a loser in this case. It appears now that vigilantism is not against the law, at least in some minds. And that's a terrifying thought.

PAMELA BOZANICH,
DISTRICT ATTORNEY AND LEAD PROSECUTOR
IN THE FIRST LYLE AND ERIK MENENDEZ MURDER TRIAL

We find the defendants incredibly guilty.

FOREMAN RETURNING JURY'S VERDICT
ON MAX BIALYSTOCK AND LEO BLOOM IN
THE FILM THE PRODUCERS

In America, an acquittal doesn't mean you're innocent. It means you beat the rap. My clients lose even when they win.

F. LEE BAILEY,
AMERICAN LAWYER

When we let the victim's personal feelings affect the judge's sentence we are reverting to a government not of laws, but of men.

HILLER B. ZOBEL,
AMERICAN JUDGE

If it doesn't fit, you must acquit.

JOHNNIE COCHRAN,
DEFENSE ATTORNEY IN THE O.J. SIMPSON TRIAL

We came here in search of justice. You will have to be the judge as to whether or not any of us found it today. But I'm not bitter and I'm not angry.

CHRISTOPHER DARDEN,
PROSECUTOR IN THE O.J. SIMPSON TRIAL
AFTER SIMPSON WAS ACQUITTED

It is clear to me that this was an emotional trial and apparently their [the jury's] decision was based on emotion that overcame reason.

GIL GARCETTI,
LOS ANGELES DISTRICT ATTORNEY
AFTER O.J. SIMPSON WAS ACQUITTED OF MURDER

Coke and Bull Story

During an Oakland County (California) drug trial in 1990, defendant Christopher Plovic claimed that he had been searched improperly by the police. While proving his point, he handed his jacket to Judge Barry Howard.

To everyone's surprise, Judge Howard pulled out a packet of cocaine from Plovic's jacket pocket. Declared the judge, "The only thing comparable is giving a speech at your high school reunion and not realizing your zipper is down."

Coughing Up Courtroom Confusion

A courtroom cough nearly sent an innocent man to prison in Wales because the judge misheard the verdict.

In 1999, Alan Rashid, 32, was being tried with making a deadly threat. As the foreman of the jury at Cardiff Crown Court rose to deliver a "not guilty" verdict, a fellow juror cleared his throat.

Judge Michael Gibbon clearly heard "guilty" but the "not" was obscured by the cough, so he sentenced Rashid to two years in prison. As Rashid was escorted to his cell to begin his sentence, a confused juror asked the bailiff why the defendant had been jailed after being found not guilty.

Until the juror spoke up, his colleagues had thought Rashid was being sentenced for another crime. The attorneys and the judge then huddled with the court reporter to correct the injustice.

In a case believed to be the first of its kind in Britain, Rashid was led back to the dock and told by Judge Gibbon that he was free to go.

CLOSING ARGUMENTS

THE PROFESSION

Any culture that has had its Jeffersons, Lincolns, and Darrows also must have a healthy notion of the lawyer's role in society.

MATTHEW A. HODEL,
AMERICAN LAWYER

Ours is a learned profession, not a mere money-getting trade.

AMERICAN BAR ASSOCIATION COMMITTEE ON PROFESSIONAL ETHICS AND GRIEVANCES, 1943

I have watched with great sadness the decline in esteem held by our society of lawyers. There must be a rediscovery of civility in the profession.

SANDRA DAY O'CONNOR,
SUPREME COURT JUSTICE

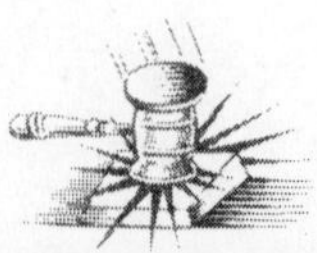

Those who are concerned about the public image of our profession would do well to look at some of this shoddy advertising.

EDWARD F. SHEA, JR.,
AMERICAN LAWYER

Lawyers are given a place of privilege in this society. They are allowed to toil in the majestic edifice of law. This provides them with dignity, challenging work, social power—and often an excellent income. For those privileges, the least they can do is behave with respect toward the institution that gives meaning to their lives: the law.

JOSEPH A. WAPNER,
JUDGE OF THE TELEVISION SHOW
THE PEOPLE'S COURT

Any profession that suffers from so foul a reputation must, in some way, provoke it.

ALAN DERSHOWITZ,
LAWYER AND HARVARD LAW PROFESSOR

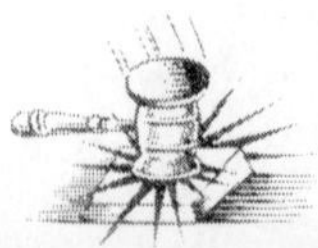

To a large extent, lawyers have shed traditional professional qualities, and the law has become an ordinary trade whose success is measured by profits.

PETER BROWN,
AMERICAN LAWYER

My generation and those older than I looked at law as a profession. Too many of the younger ones look at law as a business.

PAMELA ANN RYMER,
LOS ANGELES FEDERAL JUDGE

Lawyer bashing is almost as American as apple pie; everyone knows a good lawyer joke. And for every good lawyer joke, everyone probably knows at least one bad lawyer.

TODD GREER, LAW STUDENT,
UNIVERSITY OF ARKANSAS

Lawyers as a group are no more dedicated to justice
or public service than a private public utility
is dedicated to giving light.

DAVID MELINKOFF,
LAW PROFESSOR, UCLA

No other profession is subject to the public contempt
and derision that sometimes befalls lawyers . . .
the bitter fruit of public incomprehension
of the law itself and its dynamics.

IRVING R. KAUFMAN,
U.S. COURT OF APPEALS JUDGE

Doctors . . . still retain a high degree of public
confidence because they are perceived as healers.
Should lawyers not be healers? Healers, not warriors?
Healers, not procurers? Healers, not hired guns?

WARREN BURGER,
SUPREME COURT JUSTICE

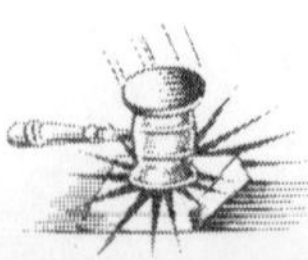

More Americans are terrified of being bit, bashed, or brutalized by attorneys. No wonder they vent their anxiety in cathartic one-liners. Should we non-lawyers stop telling the one about the skid marks, or the good start, or the researchers who turned to dissecting lawyers because they got emotionally attached to white rats?

WALTER K. OLSON,
SENIOR FELLOW, MANHATTAN INSTITUTE

It is pretty hard to find a group less concerned with serving society and more concerned with serving themselves than the lawyers.

FRED RODELL,
LAW PROFESSOR, YALE UNIVERSITY

Lawyers are like beavers:
they get in the mainstream and dam it up.

JOHN NAISBITT,
AMERICAN WRITER

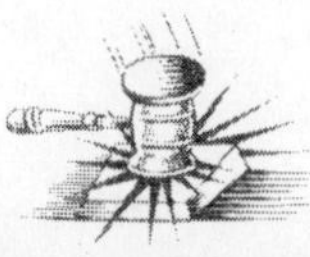

It's not a profession at all, but rather
a business service station and repair shop.

ADLAI E. STEVENSON,
AMERICAN LAWYER AND DIPLOMAT

The law is the only profession which records
its mistakes carefully, exactly as they occurred,
and yet does not identify them as mistakes.

ELLIOTT DUNLAP SMITH,
AMERICAN WRITER

Nothing could be more boring than an absolutely
accurate movie about the law.

ROGER EBERT,
AMERICAN FILM CRITIC

If it's the last thing I do, I'll put you out of business.
There must be a law even for lawyers.

LANA TURNER AS CORA SMITH,
IN THE FILM *THE POSTMAN ALWAYS RINGS TWICE*

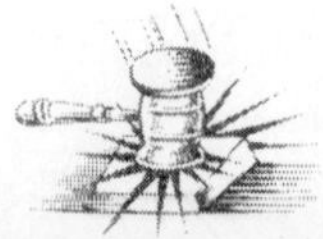

Of course had you gone to law school like your father and I wanted you to, your behavior would've been legal.

MOTHER TALKING TO CONVICT SON IN JAIL, IN CARTOONIST WILEY'S STRIP NON SEQUITUR

As a profession we have become afraid of our clients, much like parents who don't discipline their children.

JOE CONDO, AMERICAN LAWYER

The business of the law is to make sense of the confusion of what we call human life—to reduce it to order but at the same time to give it possibility, scope, even dignity.

ARCHIBALD MACLEISH, AMERICAN POET

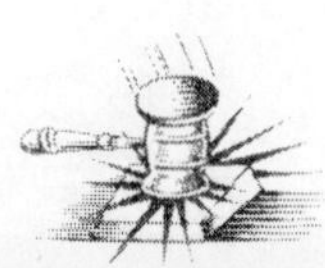

Ambition within our profession clearly has the potential to take on an addictive nature.

MIKE PAPANTONIO,
AMERICAN LAWYER

It is hard to say whether the doctors of law or of divinity have made the greater advances in the lucrative business of mystery.

SAMUEL GOLDWYN,
MOVIE PRODUCER

Personally, I don't think you can make a lawyer honest by an act of legislature. You've got to work on his conscience. And his lack of a conscience is what makes him a lawyer.

WILL ROGERS,
AMERICAN HUMORIST

Of course I've got lawyers. They are like nuclear weapons. I've got 'em 'cuz everyone else has 'em. But as soon as you use 'em, they mess everything up."

**DANNY DE VITO AS LAWRENCE GARFIELD,
CORPORATE RAIDER IN THE FILM OTHER PEOPLE'S MONEY**

It's time filmmakers get off their high horse and start treating attorneys fairly and the law honestly. Only then will the public come to understand that perhaps the law is not an ass, nor likewise its practitioners.

**ANONYMOUS ATTORNEY,
ON-LINE MAGAZINE TILT**

The law is half-assed, but it's better than working like a horse for minimum wage.

**ANONYMOUS ATTORNEY,
ON-LINE MAGAZINE TILT**

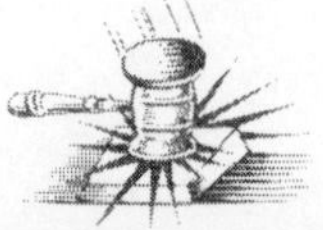

Legalese persists for a lot of bad reasons—habit, inertia, fear of change, the overwhelming influence of poorly written opinions and forms, false notions of prestige, and any number of myths about plain language. . . . There are enormous social costs of poor legal and official writing.

JOSEPH KIMBLE,
PROFESSOR, THOMAS M. COOLEY LAW SCHOOL

Lawyers who use plain language know it doesn't just make good sense, it makes good cents.

CHRISTOPHER BALMFORD,
AUSTRALIAN LAWYER

Thanks, Mom

Arnold Berwick worked hard to build up his law practice and earn the respect of his peers and his clients. When his father passed away, Berwick took over his mother's financial affairs, handling her investments and paying her bills.

One day in 1970 in Saratoga, California, she let her son know how much she appreciated his help. "It's so nice that you're taking care of everything for me," she told him "Otherwise, I'd have to hire a real attorney."

No Respect

Public defenders don't get any respect. While working as an assistant state's attorney in Marathon, Florida, Omar Hechavarria received a telephone call that left him scratching his head and laughing at the same time.

On the other end of the line was a woman who wanted to speak to the "public offender."

Mark A. Cooper, a public defender in Punta Gorda, Florida, was about to sign a pre-sentence investigation report when he noticed a slight mistake. The report had listed him as a "Public Defendant."

And Now the Good News . . .

To help restore the poor public image of the legal profession, a Beverly Hills newspaper came up with a new feature in 1989 and asked for readers' assistance.

"We would be most grateful to receive any good news about things the lawyers have done, and we promise to print them in this new column," said the paper.

The editors waited and waited for someone, anyone, to respond. Exasperated, the paper finally squashed its own idea by running the headline, "Great Deeds by the Attorneys" over an empty space.

A is for Absurd

Everyone who has scanned the Yellow Pages knows the lengths to which businesses will go to get the first listing in their category. Attorneys have tried to get into the act too. For example:

- A *Abiding Aggressive Attorney Doug Andrews*, Savannah, Georgia
- A *Guy Who's a Lawyer*, Joseph K. Luby
- A. *Aardvark Accidents Advocacy Office of Cahen, Stephen*, P.A., Miami
- AAA *Able And Willing Attorneys*, West Palm Beach, Florida

LEGAL FEES

A lawyer's opinion is worth nothing unless paid for.

ENGLISH PROVERB

Lawyer to potential client: You have a pretty good case, Mr. Pitkin. How much justice can you afford?

CARTOON CAPTION BY J.B. HANDELSMAN, THE NEW YORKER

It is not unprofessional to give free legal advice, but advertising that the first visit will be free is a bit like a fox telling chickens he will not bite them until they cross the threshold of the henhouse.

WARREN BURGER, SUPREME COURT JUSTICE

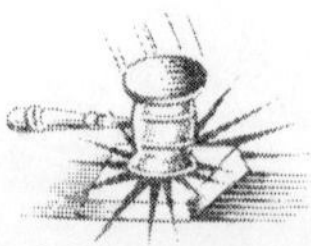

A man may as well open an oyster without
a knife, as a lawyer's mouth without a fee.

BARTEN HOLYDAY,
17TH-CENTURY ENGLISH TRANSLATOR

A shell for thee
And a shell for thee
But the oyster is the lawyer's fee.

THOMAS LEWIS INGRAM

Doctors purge the body, preachers the
conscience, lawyers the purse.

GERMAN PROVERB

Do you mean to say I would be more noble
if I charged less? Where's the nobility in that?

RICHARD ISRAELS,
CANADIAN LAWYER

The public needs the equivalent
of Chevrolets as well as Cadillacs.

LEARNED HAND,
U.S. COURT OF APPEALS JUDGE,
ON THE TREND TOWARD
POPULAR MARKETING OF LEGAL SERVICES

I can think of no other business where you are rewarded for inefficiency. No matter what you sell, the fewer hours of labor that go into the product, the more you make. With lawyers it's backwards—the more time you take, the more inefficient you are, the greater your profit.

ALAN LIEBOWITZ,
LAW FIRM AUDITOR

It seems for a lot of lawyers,
padding the bill is a creative challenge.

DIANE SAWYER,
AMERICAN TELEVISION JOURNALIST

Always remember that when you go into an attorney's office, you will have to pay for it, first or last.

ANTHONY TROLLOPE,
19TH-CENTURY ENGLISH WRITER

Lawyers charge a fortune to handle a bond offering. You know what it takes to handle a bond offering? The mental capabilities of a filing cabinet.

JIMMY BRESLIN,
AMERICAN WRITER

The practice of law is necessarily intertwined with the commercial world. Legal services should be modern, efficient and competitively priced, but they shouldn't be driven by the same bottom-line principles of the corporate world.

JEFF STEMPLE,
LAW PROFESSOR, FLORIDA STATE UNIVERSITY

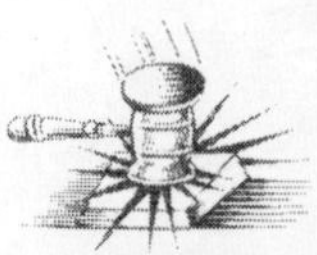

We never lose. That's why we charge a lot.

LUCY LIU AS LING WOO,
ATTORNEY IN THE TELEVISION SHOW ALLY MCBEAL

All one has to do is read the papers and see how lawyers rightly or wrongly are criticized for lots of things, not the least of which are the fees they earn.

ARTHUR F. GOLDEN,
AMERICAN LAWYER

The Buck Stops Here

As a young lawyer working on his first big case, Keith C. Rennie was sitting in Federal District Court watching a prominent attorney question a witness. The attorney was trying, unsuccessfully, to elicit certain information. Finally the judge turned to the witness and asked a question that prompted the appropriate response.

"Thank you, Your Honor," the attorney said. "How is

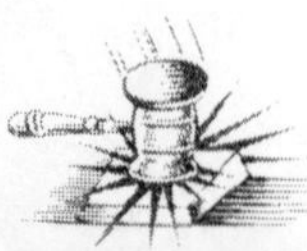

it that you were able to get to the crux of the matter with one question after I had tried three times?"

"Easy," replied the judge. "I'm not paid by the hour."

Advice and Dissent

Orville Isom was a quintessential country lawyer who practiced in Cedar City, Utah, from the 1930s to the 1980s.

If a client couldn't afford the normal fee, Isom would lower it, waive it, or trade his legal work for goods and services.

One day a man who owed a debt came into Isom's office for legal advice. Isom told the client that technically he could get out of the obligation. "But morally you have a responsibility," the lawyer added. "As legal counsel, my recommendation is that you satisfy the debt."

The client rose and walked toward the door.

"Sir, there's a $25 fee for my advice," Isom reminded him.

With a shake of his head, the man replied, "I'm not taking your advice."

So St. Peter Says to the Lawyer . . .

In a 1980 gender discrimination case involving lawyers' fees in the District of Columbia, federal district court judge Malcolm Wilkey told the following joke in his dissenting opinion:

"An immediately deceased lawyer arrived at the Pearly Gates to seek admittance from St. Peter. The Keeper of the Keys was surprisingly warm in his welcome: 'We are so glad to see you. We are particularly happy to have you here, not only because we get so few lawyers up here, but because you lived to the wonderful age of 165.' [The lawyer] was a bit doubtful and hesitant. 'Now, St. Peter, if there's one place I don't want to get into under false pretenses, it's Heaven. I really died at age 78.' St. Peter looked perplexed, frowned, and consulted the scroll in his hand. 'Ah, I see where we made our mistake as to your age. We just added up your time sheets!'"

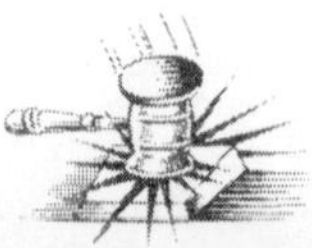

COURTROOM PERFORMANCE

[A lawyer's] performance in the courtroom is responsible for about 25 percent of the outcome; the remaining 75 percent depends on the facts.

MELVIN BELLI,
AMERICAN LAWYER

Yes, there's such a thing as luck in trial law but it only comes at 3 o'clock in the morning . . . . You'll still find me in the library looking for luck at 3 o'clock in the morning.

LOUIS NIZER,
AMERICAN LAWYER

A criminal lawyer, like a trapeze performer, is seldom more than one slip from an awful fall.

PAUL O'NEIL,
AMERICAN WRITER AND JOURNALIST

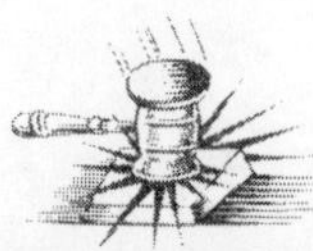

Okay, it's smoke and mirrors. So what?
You'd be surprised how much of the legal process
is exactly that. Just like in Hollywood, image
is everything in the courtroom, dahhhling.

DARLENE RICKER,
AMERICAN LAWYER AND LEGAL JOURNALIST

As long as I'm in that courtroom and I feel afraid,
it means there's something in me that's contagious.
If I didn't give a damn, I wouldn't be afraid.
Fear is a wonderful emotion.

GERRY SPENCE,
AMERICAN LAWYER

The power of clear statement
is the great power at the bar.

DANIEL WEBSTER,
18TH-CENTURY AMERICAN STATESMAN,
ORATOR, AND LAWYER

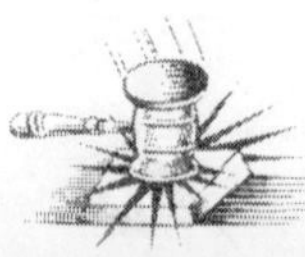

One cool judgment is worth a thousand hasty counsels.
The thing to be supplied is light, not heat.

WOODROW WILSON,
28TH PRESIDENT OF THE UNITED STATES

There are times when it's not the thrill of
winning. It's the fear of losing.

ROY BLACK,
AMERICAN LAWYER

Liars are like snakes. Sooner or later
they shed their skin. The cross-examiner's job
is to make a few small incisions that will help
them do this right in front of the jury.
Cross-examination is a process in which
you loosen the witness's skin.

MIKE FICARO,
AMERICAN LAWYER

In hard-fought litigation where the stakes are high, lawyers say and do a helluva lot of things in anger, and only a psycho would view it as heinous! You're not injuring anyone physically. You're not stealing their money. What's the big problem?

MORTON GALANE,
AMERICAN LAWYER

I'm a hunter, a combatant in the courtroom. It's just like the forest: I walk through quietly but resolutely, ready to make a purposeful kill. You must have great love to kill, to combat, to advocate.

GERRY SPENCE,
AMERICAN LAWYER

Trial work requires a computer mind that is rapid in the challenge and response. It's like live TV with no rerun. Not everyone has a mental fast ball and those who don't shouldn't try cases.

NED GOOD,
AMERICAN LAWYER

They [prosecutors] can make Mother Theresa look like a whore. That's what they're paid for.

LINDA COONEY,
FLORIDA HOUSEWIFE ACQUITTED OF MURDERING HER HUSBAND

Most of the great trial lawyers I know are very, very scared. Fear, for an actor, stirs you to a greater performance.

ARTHUR LINMAN,
AMERICAN LAWYER

Our small group of lawyers was up against perhaps the most intense investigation in the history of criminal justice. If we did not have adequate resources, we wouldn't have been able to [win].

ROBERT SHAPIRO,
DEFENSE ATTORNEY IN THE O.J. SIMPSON TRIAL

A criminal trial is like a Russian novel. It starts with exasperating slowness as the characters are introduced to a jury, then there are complications in the form of minor witnesses, the protagonist finally appears and contradictions arise to produce drama, and finally as both jury and spectators grow weary and confused the pace quickens, reaching its climax in passionate final argument.

CLIFFORD IRVING,
AMERICAN AUTHOR

Lawyers have been known to wrest from reluctant juries triumphant verdicts of acquittal for their clients, even when those clients, as often happens, were clearly and unmistakably innocent.

OSCAR WILDE,
IRISH WRITER

Lawyers may often do well, but not often by doing good . . . even when they try.

CHARLES E. SHERMAN,
AMERICAN LAWYER

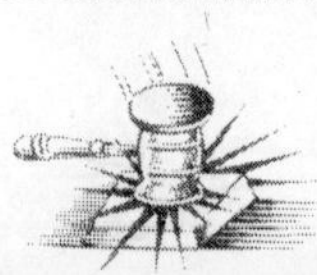

Lawyers earn a living by the sweat of browbeating others.

JAMES GIBBONS HANEKER,

Too many lawyers use words on steroids—artificially puffed-up ways of expressing ideas."

BRYAN A. GARNER,
EDITOR-IN-CHIEF, BLACK'S LAW DICTIONARY

. . . And No Dessert, Either

In the eyes of some juries, the plaintiffs and defendants act like a bunch of spoiled children.

Such was the case in Jasper, Georgia, in 1997 when a man was on trial for disorderly conduct after calling a tax assessor a liar.

Refusing to render a verdict in the case, the annoyed jury issued a statement that read: "We strongly feel that all parties involved in this case should be sent to bed without supper and not allowed to watch television for a week."

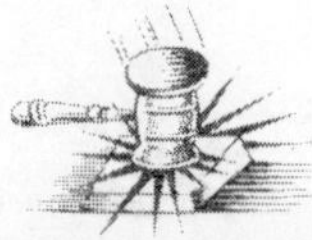

Plaid Plead

While covering a trial in 1970, Seattle reporter Eldon Barrett arrived in Superior Court Judge Henry Clay Agnew's court wearing a bright-red, Scotch-plaid jacket.

Midway through the afternoon session, Agnew, who was known for running a conservative courtroom, beckoned Barrett to the bench. In a resounding whisper, the judge told the reporter, "Next time, wear something less loud in court."

"But, Your Honor," Barrett replied smugly, "I thought Justice was blind."

"She is, young man," Agnew said. "But not by any stretch of the imagination is she deaf."

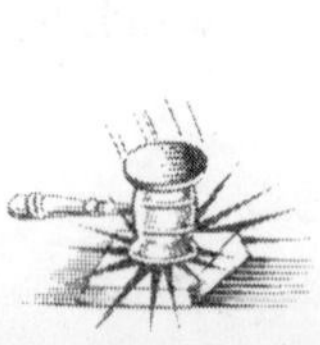

A Sick Defense

Near the end of a lengthy bench trial in federal district court in Chicago in 1986, defense attorney William Levinson moved for a new trial—because of his own inadequate representation.

In the judge's chambers, Levinson labeled his direct examination of his client "a horror." The attorney claimed it was because he was suffering from the flu.

Presiding Judge Ann Williams denied the ill-founded motion.

THE SYSTEM

I have spent all my life under a Communist regime, and I will tell you that a society without any objective legal scale is a terrible one indeed. But a society with no other scale but the legal one is not quite worthy of man either.

ALEXANDER SOLZHENITSYN,
RUSSIAN WRITER

Adversary procedure has served as a guardian of individual liberty since its inception.

STEPHAN LANDSMAN,
LAW PROFESSOR, MARSHALL COLLEGE

The legal system is often a mystery, and we, its priests, preside over rituals baffling to everyday citizens.

HENRY G. MILLER,
PRESIDENT, NEW YORK STATE BAR ASSOCIATION

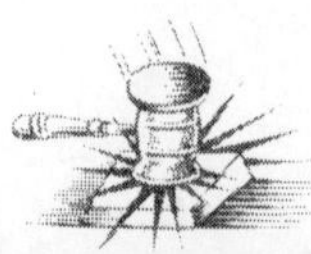

When Americans leave a courtroom feeling that their cries have been heard, we should all share pride in the fact that our legal system works as well as it does.

JOSEPH A. WAPNER,
JUDGE OF THE TELEVISION SHOW
THE PEOPLE'S COURT

In Germany, under the law everything is prohibited except that which is permitted. In France, under the law everything is permitted except that which is prohibited. In the Soviet Union, everything is prohibited, including that which is permitted. And in Italy, under the law everything is permitted, especially that which is prohibited.

NEWTON MINOW,
FCC CHAIRMAN AND LAWYER

Of course there's a different law for the rich and the poor; otherwise, who would go into business?

E. RALPH STEWART

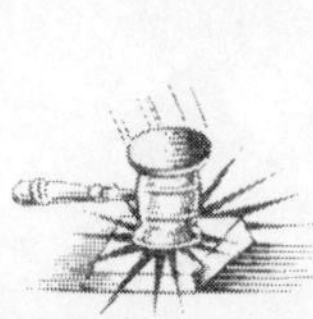

If one man can be allowed to determine for himself what is law, every man can. That means first chaos, then tyranny. Legal process is an essential part of the democratic process.

FELIX FRANKFURTER,
SUPREME COURT JUSTICE

The judicial system is the most expensive machine ever invented for finding out what happened and what to do about it.

IRVING R. KAUFMAN,
U.S. COURT OF APPEALS JUDGE

Before going to prison I believed that criticism of the criminal justice system for its treatment of the poor was so much liberal bleating and bunk. I was wrong.

G. GORDON LIDDY,
CONVICTED NIXON PRESIDENTIAL AIDE

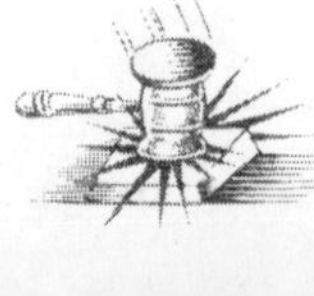

This is what has to be remembered about the law: Beneath that cold, harsh, impersonal exterior there beats a cold, harsh, impersonal heart.

DAVID FROST,
BRITISH TELEVISION JOURNALIST

The law is above the law, you know.

DOROTHY SALISBURY DAVIS,
AMERICAN WRITER

If I did half of the things this sorry President [Nixon] did, they would put me under the jail and send every key to the moon. They have the little punishments for the big men and the heavy chastisement for the poor.

RUTH SHAYS,
QUOTED IN JOHN GWALTNEY'S DRYLONGSO

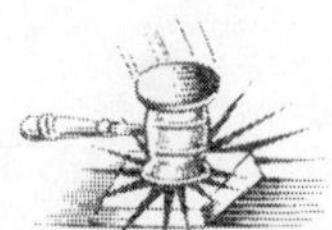

The United States is the greatest law factory
the world has ever known.

CHARLES EVANS HUGHES,
SUPREME COURT JUSTICE

As tort law operates now, it is more like a lottery
than like a rational system of justice.

MICHAEL KINSLEY,
AMERICAN JOURNALIST

Our system of civil justice is, at times,
a self-inflicted competitive disadvantage.

J. DANFORTH QUAYLE,
44TH VICE PRESIDENT OF THE UNITED STATES

We're doing this whole thing backward. Attorneys should
wear numbers on their backs, and box scores should
have entries for writs, dispositions, and appeals.

BILL VEECK,
OWNER, CHICAGO WHITE SOX

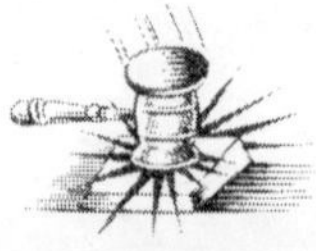

It is better to risk saving a guilty man than to condemn an innocent one.

VOLTAIRE,
17TH-CENTURY FRENCH WRITER

People say law but they mean wealth.

RALPH WALDO EMERSON,
19TH-CENTURY AMERICAN WRITER AND POET

I use the rules to frustrate the law.
But I didn't set up the ground rules.

F. LEE BAILEY,
AMERICAN LAWYER

This case proves that our justice system works—if you have the money and the influence to go all the way.

ROBERT ARUM,
LAWYER AND LONGTIME ASSOCIATE OF MUHAMMAD ALI, WHEN THE SUPREME COURT REVERSED ALI'S CONVICTION FOR DRAFT EVASION

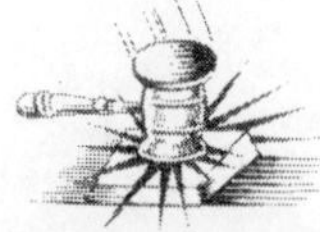

There is far too much law for those who can afford it and far too little for those who cannot.

DEREK C. BOK,
PRESIDENT, HARVARD UNIVERSITY

In law, nothing is certain but the expense.

SAMUEL BUTLER,
17TH-CENTURY ENGLISH WRITER

Laws grind the poor, and rich men rule the law.

OLIVER GOLDSMITH,
18TH-CENTURY ENGLISH WRITER

A poor man may still be able to get into heaven, but after Reaganization, he may not be able to get into court.

JANE BRYANT QUINN,
AMERICAN JOURNALIST

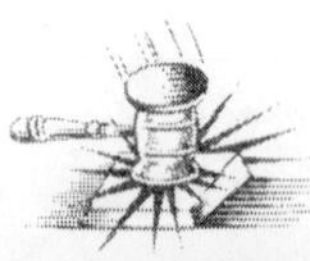

An incompetent attorney can delay a trial for years or months. A competent attorney can delay one even longer.

EVELLE J. YOUNGER,
AMERICAN LAWYER

America is the paradise of lawyers.

DAVID J. BREWER,
SUPREME COURT JUSTICE

Woman was and is condemned to a system under which the lawful rapes exceed the unlawful ones a million to one.

MARGARET SANGER,
AMERICAN POLITICAL ACTIVIST

Law is a reflection and a source of prejudice. It both enforces and suggests forms of bias.

DIANE B. SCHULDER,
AMERICAN LAWYER AND EDUCATOR

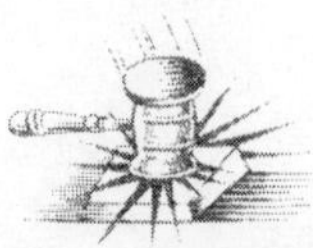

I wept for this little girl's lost childhood.
I wept for Thomas Jefferson, George Washington,
John Adams and all of our brave forefathers. . . .
And most of all, I wept for the fact that our laws have become an object of disrespect, a paper tiger that no longer insures or gives adequate redress to the most elemental right of all to live in peace and relative freedom from fear of those who would violate those laws.

EDWARD A. MILLER,
FLORIDA JUDGE,
AFTER BEING FORCED BY LAW TO REDUCE
A RAPIST'S SENTENCE IN 1993

The plain truth of the matter is that rather than alter a system that has now proven without a doubt to be incapable of dealing with crime, our society has altered itself and ignored the problem by sticking our heads in the sand like the proverbial ostrich until he wound up in the belly of a lion.

EDWARD A. MILLER,
FLORIDA JUDGE,
IN A 1993 LETTER TO THE EDITOR WHICH LED
TO A REPRIMAND FROM THE FLORIDA SUPREME COURT

It isn't the bad lawyers who are screwing up the justice system in this country, it's the good lawyers. If you have two competent lawyers on opposite sides, a trial that should take three days could easily last six months.

ART BUCHWALD,
AMERICAN JOURNALIST

Ours is a prostitute society. The system of justice, and most especially the legal profession, is a whorehouse serving those best able to afford the luxuries of justice offered to preferred customers. The lawyer, in these terms, is analogous to a prostitute. The difference between the two is simple. The prostitute is honest—the buck is her aim. The lawyer is dishonest—he claims that justice, service to mankind is his primary purpose. The lawyer's deception of the people springs from his actual money-making role; he represents the client who puts the highest fee on the table.

FLORYNCE RAE KENNEDY,
AMERICAN LAWYER AND CIVIL RIGHTS ACTIVIST

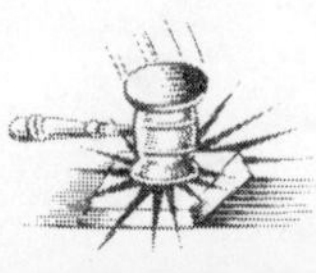

Justice is a system of revenge wherein
the State imitates the criminal.

ELBERT HUBBARD,
AMERICAN WRITER AND EDITOR

To be a trial lawyer is to see the ignominy of slow justice in a system in which the process itself punishes all who come in contact with it—the winner as well as the loser.

JOHN A. JENKINS,
JOURNALIST AND LEGAL WRITER

I cannot believe that a republic could hope to exist at the present time, if the influence of lawyers in public business did not increase in proportion to the power of the people.

ALEXIS DE TOCQUEVILLE,
19TH-CENTURY FRENCH STATESMAN AND WRITER

We've produced a system of ending disputes rather than digging up truths.

THOMAS H. ALLEN,
AMERICAN LAWYER

By the argument of counsel it was shown that at half-past ten in the morning on the day of the murder, . . . [the defendant] became insane, and remained so for eleven hours and a half exactly.

MARK TWAIN,
AMERICAN WRITER AND HUMORIST,
COMMENTING ON THE INSANITY DEFENSE

I think the law became an ass the day it let the psychiatrists get their hands on it.

LYNN COMPTON,
LOS ANGELES CHIEF DEPUTY DISTRICT ATTORNEY,
AT THE SUMMATION OF SIRHAN SIRHAN'S TRIAL
FOR ASSASSINATING ROBERT F. KENNEDY

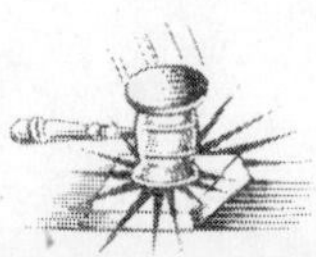

An appeal, Hinnissy, is where ye ask wan coort to show its contempt f'r another coort.

MR. DOOLEY [FINLEY PETER DUNNE], AMERICAN HUMORIST

Please don't let this [not guilty verdict] make you lose faith in our system. Please don't let this deter you from doing a job you're so well qualified to do.

MARCIA CLARK, LEAD PROSECUTOR IN THE O.J. SIMPSON TRIAL TO HER FELLOW ATTORNEYS

The impeachment power is like the ax behind the glass that says, "Do Not Break Except in Case of Emergency."

ALAN DERSHOWITZ, LAW PROFESSOR, HARVARD UNIVERSITY

Prisons are built with stones of Law.

WILLIAM BLAKE,
19TH-CENTURY ENGLISH POET

People resent that O.J. got himself in trouble, and then trashed the nation's judicial system and racial harmony to save his hide.

FRED GRAHAM,
AMERICAN LAWYER AND JOURNALIST

Achieving "finality" in death cases, and doing so as expeditiously as possible, have become the dominant goals in death penalty jurisprudence.

MOSES W. HARRISON II,
ILLINOIS SUPREME COURT JUSTICE

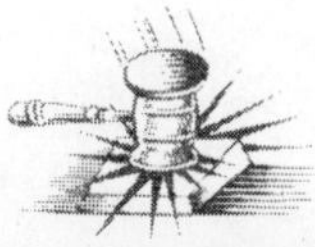

A society without any objective legal scale is a terrible one indeed. But a society with no other scale but the legal one is also less than worthy of man.

ALEKSANDR I. SOLZHENITSYN,
RUSSIAN WRITER

The bigger the system gets, the more impersonal the system gets and the less ability the judges have to hear the same thing again and again and react to it on a case-by-case basis.

DAVID ROTHMAN,
AMERICAN LAWYER

Rather than functioning as a deterrent, the criminal justice process too often operates to reinforce the offender's belief that he can commit crimes with impunity.

JAMES R. THOMPSON,
ILLINOIS GOVERNOR

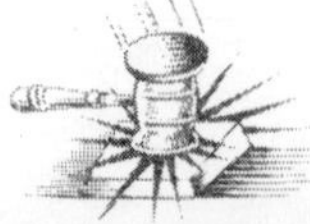

Sock it to Him

When Ed Koch was running for mayor in New York City in 1973, he went to a senior citizens center in the Bronx.

The candidate was immediately asked about crime and what he intended to do about it. "Crime is terrible," he replied. "A judge I know was mugged this week and do you know what he did? He called a press conference and said the mugging would in no way affect his judicial decisions in matters of that kind."

An elderly woman stood up and shouted, "Then mug him again!"

A Ruling that Made No Cents

After four years of legal wranglings over the ownership of some property in Palmdale, California, a settlement was finally reached in 1992—but justice was held up over a single penny.

L.A. Superior Court officials refused to let the two parties split a $30,832.81 deposit because one party would receive a penny more than the other. Attorneys from both sides offered to toss in a cent to make it even, but the officials insisted on a new formal order.

To satisfy the court finance officer, a new court order was drawn up and sent by messenger to all parties who had to appear at an early-morning special court hearing. The legal costs to resolve the one-cent issue: $1,050.

Three Tiers for the Judge

Before three justices in the Hong Kong Court of Criminal Appeals, lawyer Angus McKay gave three reasons why he felt his client's conviction should be overturned.

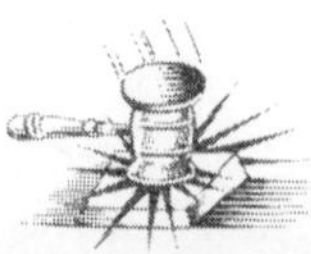

"Mr. McKay," said one of the judges, "the first tier of your case is that the identification was wrong, the second tier that the statements should have been disregarded, and the third tier is that the conviction is against the weight of evidence in any event, is that not right?"

McKay couldn't resist a clever reply: "If I have reduced your Lordship to tiers, should I really continue?"

Typos

A 1991 brief said it had an index containing an "extensive copulation of authorities."

• A 1992 court paper was addressed to "The Horable U.S. District Judge."

• A 1993 notice of appeal ended with "Rectfully submitted."

• A 1993 agricultural lease involving demised premises stated the tenant was entitled to exclusive use and possession of the "demised penises."

• A 1990 estate plan attempted a distribution of "asses."

ON REFORM

Even when laws have been written down, they ought not always to remain unaltered.

ARISTOTLE,
4TH-CENTURY B.C. GREEK PHILOSOPHER

Law is merely the expression of the will of the strongest for the time being, and therefore laws have no fixity, but shift from generation to generation.

BROOKS ADAMS,
19TH-CENTURY AMERICAN HISTORIAN

The law, like the traveler, must be ready for the morrow. It must have the principle of growth.

BENJAMIN CARDOZO,
SUPREME COURT JUSTICE

To the law we bow with reverence. It is the one king that commands our allegiance. We will change our king when his rule is oppressive.

BENJAMIN HARRISON,
23RD PRESIDENT OF THE UNITED STATES

Nothing is more subject to change than the laws.

MICHEL DE MONTAIGNE,
16TH-CENTURY FRENCH WRITER

Laws should not be changed without good reason.

CHARLES LOUIS DE MONTESQUIEU,
17TH-CENTURY FRENCH LAWYER AND POLITICAL PHILOSOPHER

When I hear any man talk of an unalterable law, the only effect it produces upon me is to convince me that he is an unalterable fool.

SYDNEY SMITH,
18TH-CENTURY ENGLISH WRITER

Somewhere "out there," beyond the walls of the courthouse, run currents and tides of public opinion which lap at the courtroom door.

WILLIAM H. REHNQUIST,
SUPREME COURT JUSTICE, ON THE PUBLIC'S INFLUENCE TO CHANGE LAWS

Law reform is far too serious a matter to be left to the legal profession.

LORD LESLIE SCARMAN,
ENGLISH LAWYER

If you got the sayso you want to keep it, whether you are right or wrong. That's why they have to keep changing the laws—so they don't unbenefit any of these big white men.

RUTH SHAYS,
QUOTED IN JOHN GWALTNEY'S DRYLONGSO

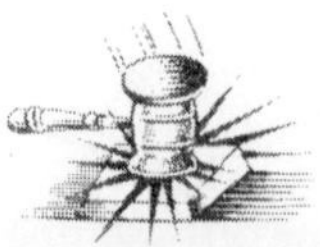

Law and justice are not always the same. When they aren't, destroying the law may be the first step toward changing it.

**GLORIA STEINEM,
AMERICAN WRITER AND FEMINIST**

We have the means to change the laws we find unjust or onerous. We cannot, as citizens, pick and choose the laws we will or will not obey.

**RONALD W. REAGAN,
40TH PRESIDENT OF THE UNITED STATES**

Laws and institutions are constantly tending to gravitate. Like clocks, they must be occasionally cleansed, and wound up, and set to true time.

**HENRY WARD BEECHER,
19TH-CENTURY AMERICAN CLERGYMAN**

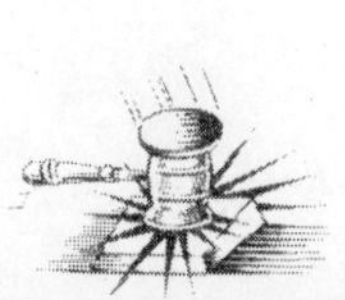

Law and equity are two things that God hath joined, but which man hath put asunder.

CHARLES C. COLTON,
18TH-CENTURY ENGLISH CLERGYMAN AND WRITER

The worse the society, the more law there will be. In Hell there will be nothing but law, and due process will be meticulously observed.

GRANT GILMORE,
LEGAL SCHOLAR

The rule of law can be wiped out in one misguided, however well-intentioned, generation.

WILLIAM T. GOSSETT,
PRESIDENT, AMERICAN BAR ASSOCIATION

New lords, new laws.

SIR JOHN HARINGTON,
16TH-CENTURY ENGLISH WRITER AND TRANSLATOR

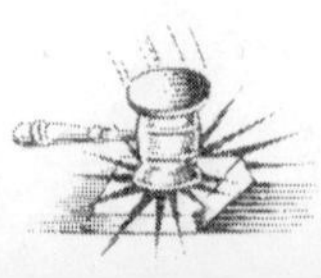

It cannot be helped, it is as it should be,
that the law is behind the times.

OLIVER WENDELL HOLMES, JR.,
SUPREME COURT JUSTICE

Law must be stable and yet it cannot stand still.

ROSCOE POUND,
DEAN EMERITUS, HARVARD LAW SCHOOL

Petty laws breed great crimes.

OUIDA,
18TH-CENTURY SCOTTISH WRITER

The law changes and flows like water,
and . . . the stream of women's rights law
has become a sudden rushing torrent.

SHANA ALEXANDER,
AMERICAN JOURNALIST

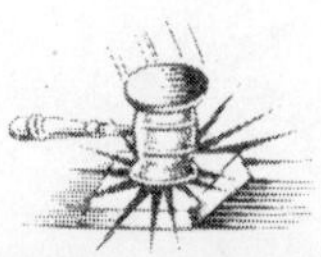

It is perfectly proper to regard and study the law simply as a great anthropological document.

OLIVER WENDELL HOLMES, JR.,
SUPREME COURT JUSTICE

Every new time will give its law.

MAXIM GORKY,
RUSSIAN WRITER

We must do more to ensure that people without resources are not disadvantaged in courts whether as civil plaintiffs or criminal defendants or even as victims.

RAY BROWN,
AMERICAN LAWYER

I do not think the state should engage in conduct that should be left to a higher power.

CATHERINE CRIER,
AMERICAN JUDGE, ON THE DEATH PENALTY

> Capital punishment would be more effective as a preventive measure if it were administered prior to the crime.
>
> **WOODY ALLEN,**
> **AMERICAN WRITER AND DIRECTOR**

Legaldegook

Here are some 1993 winners of the annual Legaldegook Awards, selected by the Plain Language Committee of the State Bar of Texas:

• To an attorney who claims his position is supported by a statement in an accompanying affidavit in the case file: "It all fully appears from the affidavit of the publisher heretofore herein filed."

• To an attorney who writes that the pleading may refer to other documents previously filed: "The Court may take judicial notice of such pleadings which are on file herein and such pleadings are incorporated herein by reference and made a part hereof as if copied here in full."

Who Do You Trust?

When Miami lawyer Stephen Nagin received a call one day in 1991 from a potential client who wanted a divorce, he was perplexed because he specialized in antitrust suits.

"Why would you call me?" he asked the woman caller.

"Well," she replied, "I saw your name in the Yellow Pages under antitrust lawyers, and I don't trust my husband."

Nagin respectfully declined to represent her.

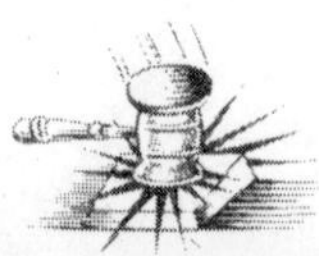

ADVICE TO LAWYERS

I'll tell you what my daddy told me after my first trial. I thought I was just great. I asked him, "How did I do?" He paused and said, "You've got to guard against speaking more clearly than you think."

HOWARD H. BAKER, JR., UNITED STATES SENATOR

You don't approach a case with the philosophy of applying abstract justice—you go in to win.

PERCY FOREMAN, AMERICAN LAWYER

Be concise for clients. Less is more. Bravura displays only serve to irritate; brevity is what pays the rent.

JAMES C. FREUND, AMERICAN LAWYER

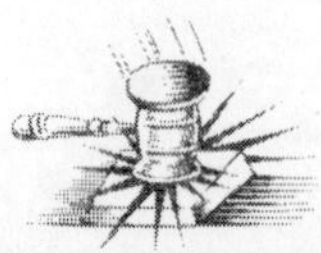

Be you never so high, the law is above you.

THOMAS FULLER,
17TH-CENTURY ENGLISH WRITER

When you have the facts on your side,
argue the facts. When you have the law on your side,
argue the law. When you have neither, holler.

ALBERT GORE, JR.,
45TH VICE PRESIDENT OF THE UNITED STATES

When you have no basis for an argument,
abuse the plaintiff.

CICERO,
1ST-CENTURY B.C. ROMAN STATESMAN,
ORATOR, AND WRITER

My thesis is that the truly successful lawyer
finds a good heart more useful than sharp fangs.

MATTHEW A. HODEL,
AMERICAN LAWYER

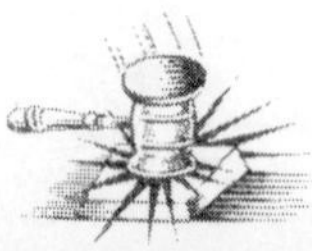

There is a vague popular belief that lawyers are necessarily dishonest. I say vague, because when we consider to what extent confidence and honors are reposed in and conferred upon lawyers by the people, it appears improbable that their impression of dishonesty is very distinct and vivid. Yet the impression is common, almost universal. Let no young man choosing the law for a calling for a moment yield to the popular belief—resolve to be honest at all events; and if in your own judgment you cannot be an honest lawyer, resolve to be honest without being a lawyer. Choose some other occupation, rather than one in the choosing of which you do, in advance, consent to be a knave.

ABRAHAM LINCOLN,
16TH PRESIDENT OF THE UNITED STATES

In university they don't tell you that the greater part of the law is learning to tolerate fools.

DORIS LESSING,
ENGLISH WRITER

I used to say that, as Solicitor General, I made three arguments of every case. First came the one that I planned as I thought—logical, coherent, complete. Second was the one actually presented—interrupted, incoherent, disjointed, disappointing. The third was the utterly devastating argument that I thought of after going to bed that night.

ROBERT H. JACKSON,
SUPREME COURT JUSTICE

Never, never, never, on cross examination, ask a witness a question you don't already know the answer to, was a tenet I absorbed with my baby food. Do it, and you'll often get an answer you don't want.

ATTICUS FINCH,
IN HARPER LEE'S TO KILL A MOCKINGBIRD

[Preparation] is the be-all of good trial work. Everything else—felicity of expression, improvisational brilliance—is a satellite around the sun. Thorough preparation is that sun.

LOUIS NIZER,
AMERICAN LAWYER

People don't ordinarily look forward to starting at the bottom. While you may be a lowly foot soldier . . . no one knows more about solving a problem than the person at the bottom.

SANDRA DAY O'CONNOR,
SUPREME COURT JUSTICE,
RECALLING THE DAYS EARLY IN HER CAREER
IN A MALL LAW OFFICE COLLECTING
UNPAID GROCERY BILLS

There is always room at the top.

DANIEL WEBSTER,
AMERICAN STATESMAN, ORATOR, AND LAWYER,
WHEN ADVISED NOT TO BECOME
A LAWYER BECAUSE THE PROFESSION
WAS OVERCROWDED

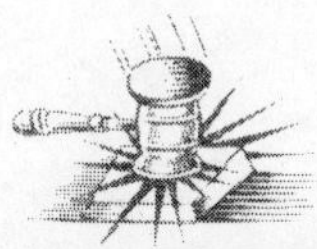

Extemporaneous speaking should be practiced and cultivated. It is the lawyer's avenue to the public.

ABRAHAM LINCOLN,
16TH PRESIDENT OF THE UNITED STATES

To find real pleasure in the legal life, you need to open yourself to all your sources of potential meaning. . . . Understanding a client beyond her present legal problem does not detract from the technical job at hand.

STEVEN KEEVA,
AMERICAN JOURNALIST

My father told me that all you need to succeed in the law is a certain amount of common sense and clean fingernails.

JOHN MORTIMER,
ENGLISH LAWYER AND WRITER

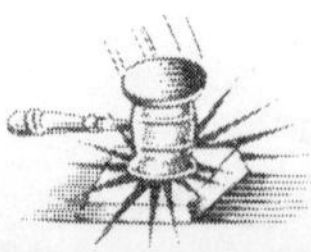

Wisdom too often never comes, and so one ought not to reject it merely because it comes too late.

FELIX FRANKFURTER,
SUPREME COURT JUSTICE

Accepting representation of another human being is a serious commitment and should always be treated as such.

WARREN ANDERSON,
AMERICAN LAWYER

Courage is the most important attribute of a lawyer. It is more important than competence or vision. It can never be an elective in any law school . . . and it should pervade the heart, the halls of justice and the chambers of the mind.

ROBERT F. KENNEDY,
U.S. ATTORNEY GENERAL

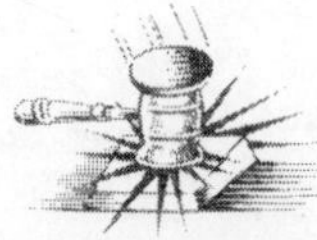

A shot glass of facts is worth a tub of law.

WILLIAM F. MCHUGH,
LAW PROFESSOR, FLORIDA STATE UNIVERSITY

When in the classroom or debating minute matters with classmates, it's perfectly fine to "think like a lawyer." But back on the outside, back in the real world, a contract is still an agreement, property is still stuff, and torts are still those fancy little pastries.

ANONYMOUS ATTORNEY,
ON-LINE MAGAZINE TILT

For a good time, hire a hooker.
For a lot of time, hire my attorney.

PRISON CELL GRAFFITI

Court in Repose

After a big lunch one day in 1989, Judge George D. Warner Jr. of the Chancery Court in Meridian, Mississippi, couldn't keep his eyes open in court. He realized he had dropped off to sleep when he cracked his eyes open and not a sound could be heard.

One lawyer was looking at him with his notes in his hand. The other lawyer questioning the witness was standing still before proceeding.

Judge Warner looked at the first lawyer and announced, "Objection sustained!"

"But, Judge, I didn't object," the lawyer said.

"Well," said the embarrassed judge, "you should have!"

INDEX OF NAMES

Abrams, Floyd (b. 1936), American lawyer, 68
Abramson, Leslie, defense attorney, 91
Adams, Brooks (1848–1927), American historian, 256
Adams, John (1735–1826), 2nd President of the United States, 132
Adler, Freda (b. 1934), American educator, 28
Adler, Renata (b. 1938), Italian-born American writer, film critic, and philosopher, 183
Aeschylus (525–456 B.C.), Greek dramatist, 153
Alexander, Shana (b. 1925), American journalist, 261
Allen, Thomas H. (b. 1945), American lawyer, 249
Allen, Woody (b. 1935), American writer and film director, 263
Anacharsis, 6th-century B.C. Scythian philosopher, 34
Anderson, Maxwell (1889–1959), American playwright, 83
Anderson, Warren, American lawyer, 271
Aquinas, St. Thomas (1225–1274), Italian theologian, 22
Arbuthnot, John (1667–1735), Scottish physician and writer, 22
Aristotle (384–322 B.C.), Greek philosopher, 22, 23, 27, 132, 256
Arum, Robert (b. 1931), American lawyer, 243
Bacon, Francis (1561–1626), English philosopher and writer, 34, 51, 82, 164
Bailey, F. Lee (b. 1933), American lawyer, 70, 98, 131, 201, 243
Baker, Howard H., Jr. (b. 1925), United States Senator, 265
Balmford, Christopher, Australian lawyer, 218
Barrett, Don, American lawyer, 200
Barrows, Sydney Biddle (b. 1952), 98
Barry, Dave (b. 1947), American syndicated columnist, 79
Baxter, William F. (b. 1929), Assistant U.S. Attorney General, 41
Beecher, Henry Ward (1813–1887), American clergyman, 21, 29, 259

Bender, Harry, 189
Belli, Melvin (b. 1907), American lawyer, 69, 122, 229
Bernard, Sidney, 100
Berry, Mary Frances (b. 1938), American legal scholar and civil rights activist, 153
Beschloss, Michael, Presidential historian, 133
Bickel, Alexander M. (1924–1974), Romanian-born American legal scholar, 29
Bierce, Ambrose (1842–1914), American writer, 52, 65, 98, 155, 189, 192
Bismarck, Otto von (1815–1898), Prussian prince, 15
Black, Hugo L. (1886–1971), Supreme Court Justice, 116
Black, Roy (b. 1945), American lawyer, 231
Blackmun, Harry A. (b. 1908), Supreme Court Justice, 68, 113, 115
Blake, William (1757–1827), 19th century English poet, 251
Bleckley, Logan E. (1827–1907), American judge, 49
Blount, Roy, Jr. (b. 1941), American writer, 137
Bohn, Henry George (1796–1884), English publisher, 71
Bok, Curtis (1897–1962), Pennsylvania Supreme Court Justice, 83
Bok, Derek C. (b. 1930), President, Harvard University, 244
Borrow, George (1803–1881), English writer and linguist, 40
Bozanich, Pamela, American lawyer, 201
Brakel, Samuel Jan, American lawyer, 123
Brandeis, Louis D. (1856–1941), Supreme Court Justice, 20, 164
Brennan, William J., Jr. (b. 1906), Supreme Court Justice, 113, 115
Breslin, Jimmy (b. 1929), American writer, 225
Brewer, David J. (1837–1910), Supreme Court Justice, 245
Brink, David R. (b. 1919), President, American Bar Association, 121
Brougham, Henry Peter (1778–1868), Scottish judge and political leader, 42
Brown, Peter (b. 1922), American lawyer, 123, 211
Brown, Ray, American lawyer, 139, 165, 196, 262
Bruce, Lenny (1926–1966), American comedian, 87
Bruyère, Jean de la (1645–1696), French writer and moralist, 89
Bryant, Ed (b. 1949), U.S Representative from Tennessee, 126
Buchwald, Art (b. 1925), American journalist, 247

Burger, Warren (b. 1907), Supreme Court Justice, 58, 184, 192, 212, 222
Burke, Edmund (1729–1797), English statesman and orator, 162, 165
Bush, George (b. 1924), 41st President of the United States, 196
Butler, Samuel (1612–1680), English satirical poet, 159, 244
Butler, Samuel (1835–1902), English writer and journalist, 48, 162
Campbell, William J. (b. 1948), U.S. District Court judge, 99
Camus, Albert (1913–1960), French writer, 162
Cardozo, Benjamin (1870–1938), Supreme Court Justice, 256
Carlyle, Jane Welsh (1801–1866), Scottish poet, 173
Carter, Rubin "Hurricane" (b. 1937), American boxer, 168
Carter, Terry, American journalist, 78
Cervantes, Miguel de (1547–1616), Spanish writer, 89
Chandler, Raymond (1888–1959), American mystery and suspense writer, 15, 166
Choak, Rufus (1799–1859), 19th-century American jurist, 91
Choate, Joseph H. (1832–1917), American lawyer and diplomat, 42
Cicero (106–43 B.C.), Roman statesman, orator, and writer, 23, 32, 158, 174, 266
Clark, Champ (1850–1921), United States Congressman, 90
Clark, Charles E. (1889–1963), U.S. Court of Appeals judge, 88
Clark, Marica (b. 1953), Lead prosecutor in the O.J. Simpson criminal trial, 250
Clark, Ramsey (b. 1927), U.S. Attorney General, 157
Coburn, Daniel (b. 1943), American lawyer, 193
Cochran, Johnnie (b. 1937), Defense Attorney in the O. J. Simpson Trial, 202
Cohen, Felix S., lawyer and legal scholar, 127
Cohen, Morris (1880–1947), Russian-born American philosopher, 23, 29
Cohn, Roy M. (1927–1986), American lawyer, 88
Colden, Cadwallader (1688–1776), British-American politician, 132
Coleridge, Samuel Taylor (1772–1834), English poet, 56
Colton, Charles C. (1780–1832), English clergyman and writer, 260
Compton, Lynn, Los Angeles Chief Deputy District Attorney, 249
Condo, Joe, 215
Conine, Ernest (b. 1925), American journalist, 183
Cook, Peter (1937–1995), British writer and entertainer, 93

Cooney, Linda, 233
Cooper, Charles J., American lawyer, 133, 150
Cooper, James Fenimore (1789–1851), American writer, 16, 99
Corboy, Philip (b. 1924), American lawyer, 40, 103
Corcoran, Barbara (b. 1911), American writer, 154
Countryman, Vernon, professor, Harvard University, 56
Cox, Archibald (b. 1912), Watergate prosecutor, 147
Cozzens, James Gould (1903–1978), American writer, 124
Cressey, Donald R. (b. 1919), American writer, 70
Crier, Catherine, American Judge, 262
Crosby, Norm (b. 1927), American comedian, 104
Cross, Amanda (b. 1926), American literary scholar and writer, 71
Cuomo, Mario (b. 1932), American politician, 115
Curtin, John J., Jr. (b. 1933), American lawyer, 41
Curtis, Charles P. (1860–1948), American lawyer, 124
Darden, Christopher (b. 1956), prosecutor in the O. J. Simpson criminal trial, 202
Darling, C. J., 19th-century English judge, 33
Darrow, Clarence (1857–1938), American lawyer and writer, 23, 39, 100,154
Dauten, Dale, American newspaper columnist, 183
Davis, Angela Yvonne (b. 1944), American civil rights activist and educator, 173
Davis, Dorothy Salisbury (b. 1916), American writer, 241
Defoe, Daniel (1660–1731), English writer, 27, 154, 161
Dershowitz, Alan (b. 1938), lawyer and Harvard law professor, 72, 84, 134, 184, 193, 210, 250
Dickens, Charles (1812–1870), English writer, 69
Diderot, Denis (1713–1784), French encyclopedist, 144
Dillwyn, Lewis W. (1788–1855), English naturalist, 184
Disraeli, Benjamin (1804–1881), British prime minister, 33, 154
Docquier, L., French aphorist, 42
Douglas, William O. (1898–1980), Supreme Court Justice, 15, 90, 148
Dudley, John, 18th-century Judge, 165
Dunne, Finley Peter (1867–1936), American humorist, 155, 250

Dworkin, Ronald D. (b. 1931), law professor, New York University, 31
Ebert, Roger (b. 1942), American film critic, 214
Einstein, Albert (1879–1955), German-born American physicist, 21
Emerson, Ralph Waldo (1803–1882), American writer and poet, 82, 144, 243
Epictetus (342–270 B.C.), Greek philosopher, 32
Erdmann, Martin, American lawyer, 82
Ervin, Samuel Jr., (1896–1985), United States Senator, 85, 131
Evarts, William (1818–1901), American lawyer, 174
Ferdinand I (1503–1564), Holy Roman Emperor, 161
Ficaro, Mike (b. 1947), American lawyer, 231
Follette, Suzanne La (b. 1893), American politician and feminist, 19
Foreman, Percy (1902–1988), American lawyer, 265
Ford, Gerald R., (b. 1913), 38th President of the United States, 135
Ford, Malcolm, 43
Fortas, Abe (1910–1982), Supreme Court Justice, 87
France, Anatole (1844–1924), French writer, 19

Francis, Henry Waldorf, 188
Frank, Jerome, American Judge, 16
Frankfurter, Felix (1882–1965), Supreme Court Justice, 240, 271
Franklin, Benjamin (1706–1790), American statesman and philosopher, 29, 50
Freund, James C. (b. 1934), American lawyer, 265
Frost, David (b. 1939), British television journalist, 241
Frost, Robert (1874–1963), American poet, 100
Fuchsberg, Jacob D. (b. 1913), President, American Trial Lawyers Association, 100
Fuller, Thomas (1608–1661), English writer, 28, 55, 266
Gaddis, William (b. 1922), writer, 162
Galane, Morton (b. 1926), American lawyer, 232
Galsworthy, John (1867–1933), English writer and dramatist, 24
Garcetti, Gil (b. 1941), Los Angeles Distrit Attorney, 203
Gardner, John W. (b. 1912), U.S. Secretary of Health, Education, and Welfare, 18
Garner, Bryan A., Editor-in-Chief, *Black's Law Dicitonary*, 235
Garrison, William Lloyd (1805–1879), American Abolitionist, 177

Gasset, Jose Ortega y (1883–1955), Spanish philosopher, 18
Gates, Bill (b. 1955), CEO of Microsoft, 196
Gerber, Ann, American journalist, 121
Gibbon, Edward (1737–1794), English historian, 28
Gilbert, William S. (1836–1911), English poet and writer, 25
Gilmore, Grant (1910–1982), legal scholar, 260
Giraudoux, Jean (1882–1944), French playwright, 125, 140
Gladstone, William E. (1809–1898), British statesman, 174
Goethe, Johann Wolfgang von (1749–1832), German poet and dramatist, 33
Golden, Arthur F. (b. 1946), American lawyer, 226
Goldsmith, Oliver (1728–1774), English writer, 49, 244
Goldwater, Barry (b. 1909), American statesmen, 166
Goldwyn, Samuel (1882–1947), film producer, 216
Good, Ned (b. 1928), American lawyer, 232
Gore, Albert, Jr. (b. 1948), 45th Vice President of the United States, 266
Gorky, Maxim (1868–1936), Russian writer, 262
Gossett, William T. (b. 1904), President, American Bar Association, 260
Graham, Fred (b. 1931), American lawyer and journalist, 251
Grant, Ulysses S. (1822–1885), 18th President of the United States, 30
Grace, Nancy, American lawyer, 50
Greebler, Arthur (b. 1956), American lawyer, 65
Greene, Lord Wilfrid Arthur (1883–1952), English judge, 66
Greer, Todd, law student, University of Arkansas, 211
Grossman, Moses Henry (1873–1942), American judge, 187
Hamilton, Alexander (1757–1804), American statesman, 194
Hand, Learned (1872–1961), U.S. Court of Appeals judge, 155, 224
Haneker, James Gibbons, 235
Harington, Sir John (1561–1612), English writer and translator, 260
Harris, Sydney J. (1917–1986), British-American writer, 124
Harrison, Benjamin (1833–1901), 23rd President of the United States, 257
Harrison, Moses W. II, (b. 1932), Illinois Supreme Court Justice, 251
Hart, Frances Noyes (1890–1943), 194

Hathaway, George (1852–1903), American writer, 43
Hays, Arthur (1881–1954), American lawyer, 48
Hellman, Lillian (1905–1984), American dramatist, 174
Hertz, Joseph H. (1872–1946), British-born Hungarian Rabbi, 163
Hinkson, Katherine T. (1861–1931), Irish poet and writer, 54
Hodel, Matthew A. (b. 1955), American lawyer, 209, 266
Hoff, Joan, Ohio University Hisorian, 134
Holmes, Oliver Wendell, Jr. (1809–1894), Supreme Court Justice, 90, 193, 261, 262
Holyday, Barten, 17th-century English translator, 223
Hooker, Richard (1554–1600), English theologian, 25
Hooks, Benjamin (b. 1925), Chairman, NAACP, 113
Hoover, J. Edgar (1895–1972), Director, FBI, 156
Horace (65–8 B.C.), Roman poet and satirist, 89, 154
Horsley, Samuel (1733–1806), English bishop, 143
Houser, Dick, 72
Hubbard, Elbert (1856–1915), American writer and editor, 47, 103, 248
Hughes, Charles Evans (1862–1948), Supreme Court Justice, 242
Humphrey, Hubert (1911–1978), 38th Vice President of the United States, 145
Hunt, Lamar (b. 1932), owner, Kansas City Chiefs football team, 46
Ingersoll, Robert G. (1844–1915), American lawyer, 156
Ingram, Thomas Lewis, 223
Irving, Clifford, American lawyer, 234
Irving, Washington (1783–1859), American writer, 50
Israels, Richard (b. 1946), Canadian lawyer, 131, 156, 223
Ito, Lance (b. 1950), judge in the O.J. Simpson trial, 92
Jackson, Jesse (b. 1941), American clergyman and civil rights leader, 157
Jackson, Robert H. (1892–1954), Supreme Court Justice, 139, 268
Jaworski, Leon (1905–1982), special prosecutor for the Watergate trials, 16
Jefferson, Thomas (1743–1826), 3rd President of the United States, 30, 84, 88, 130
Jenkins, John A., journalist and legal writer, 248
Johnson, Phillip E., (b. 1940), law professor, University of California, 125
Johnston, Neal, Chief of Staff, New York City Council, 77

Joubert, Joseph (1754–1824), French writer and moralist, 156
Justinian I (483–565), Emperor of Byzantine, 163
Kafka, Franz (1883–1924), Czechoslovakian novelist, 54
Kallen, Lucille (b. 1932), writer, 38
Katzenbach, John (b. 1950), American journalist, 57
Kaufman, Irving R. (1910–1992), U.S. Court of Appeals judge, 40, 85, 212, 240
Keats, John (1795–1821), English poet, 46
Keeva, Steven, American journalist, 270
Kellett, Christine (b. 1942), law professor, Dickinson School, 114
Kennedy, Florynce Rae (b. 1916), American lawyer and civil rights activist, 57, 247
Kennedy, John F. (1917–1963), 35th President of the United States, 160
Kennedy, Robert F. (1925–1968), U.S. Attorney General, 157, 176, 271
Kimble, Joseph, Thomas M. Cooley Law School Professor, 218
King, Dr. Martin Luther, Jr. (1929–1968), American clergyman and civil rights leader, 22, 143, 149, 175
Kinsley, Michael (b. 1951), American journalist, 242
Kissinger, Henry (b. 1923), National Security Advisor and Secretary of State, 148
Klieman, Rikki, American lawyer, 73, 104
Kumble, Steven J. (b. 1933), American lawyer, 66
Landor, Walter Savage (1775–1864), English writer, 31
Landsman, Stephan (b. 1946), law professor, Marshall College, 238
Lec, Stanislaw (1909–1966), Czech writer, 153
Lee, Harper (b. 1926), American writer, 177
Lenin, Nikolai (1870–1924), Russian revolutionary leader, 86
Leno, Jay (b. 1950), American comedian, 114
Lessing, Doris (b. 1919), English writer, 267
Liddy, G. Gordon (b. 1930), convicted Nixon presidential aide, 240
Liebowitz, Alan, law firm auditor, 224
Lillie, Charisse R. (b. 1952), Chair of the American Bar Association Commission for Opportunities for Minorities in the Profession, 52
Liman, Arthur (b. 1932), American lawyer, 233
Lincoln, Abraham (1809–1865), 16th President of the United States, 185, 188, 267, 270

Linowitz, Sol M. (b. 1913), American lawyer, 41
Locke, John (1632–1704), English philosopher, 19
Louis XII (1462–1515), King of France, 48
Lycophron, 3rd-century B.C. Greek poet and scholar, 20
Machiavelli, Niccolo (1469–1527), Italian statesman and political philosopher, 86
McGeorge, John, Australian psychiatrist, 71, 99
McHugh, William F., Law Professor, Florida State Univeristy, 272
McLaughlin, Mignon, American writer, 71
MacKinnon, Catharine (b. 1946), American law professor, feminist, and writer, 28
Macklin, Charles (1697–1797), Irish actor and dramatist, 24
MacLeish, Archibald (1892–1947), American poet, 215
Manuasa, Danny, American lawyer, 73
Marcuse, Herbert (1898–1979), German-American philosopher, 24
Mark, Robert, British police commissioner, 194
Marshall, John (1755–1835), Supreme Court Justice,
Masterson, Bert, 87
Mayer, Milton (b. 1908), American journalist, 132
Melinkoff, David (b. 1914), law professor, UCLA, 212
Melville, Herman (1819–1891), American writer, 147
Mencken, H. L. (1880–1956), American journalist, 86, 101, 175, 193
Middleton, Thomas (1570–1627), English dramatist, 161
Millay, Edna St. Vincent (1892–1950), American poet, 42
Miller, Edward A. (b. 1931), Florida judge, 246
Miller, Henry G. (b. 1931), former President, New York State Bar Association, 238
Miller, Samuel F. (1816–1890), American judge, 143
Minow, Newton (b. 1926), FCC chairman and lawyer, 101, 239
Montaigne, Michel de (1533–1592), French writer, 146, 257
Montesquieu, Charles Louis de (1689–1755), French lawyer and political philosopher, 19, 257
Moone, Hoyt, American lawyer, 77
Moore, Portia (b. 1955), American lawyer, 110
Morgan, J. P. (1837–1913), American financier, 70

Morgenthau, Robert (b. 1919), New York City District Attorney, 102
Morphonios, Ellen (b. 1929), American judge, 157
Morris, Robert J., American lawyer, 92
Morrison, Peter, American lawyer, 44
Mortimer, John (b. 1923), English lawyer and writer, 270
Myerson, Abraham (1881–1948), Russian-American neuropsychiatrist, 144
Naisbitt, John (b. 1929), American writer, 213
Napoleon I (1769–1821), Emperor of France, 24, 158
Nix, Robert N. C. (b. 1955), United States Congressman, 137
Nixon, Richard (1913–1994), 37th President of the United States, 148
Nizer, Louis (b. 1902), American lawyer, 229, 269
Nolan, John T., 67
Norris, George W. (1861–1944), United States Senator, 114
North, Christopher (1785–1854), Scottish writer, 145
North, Oliver (b. 1943), Marine Lt. Colonel, 74
O'Connor, Sandra Day (b. 1930), Supreme Court Justice, 209, 269
O'Neil, Paul (1909–1988), American writer and journalist, 44, 229
Olson, Walter K. (b. 1954), Senior fellow, Manhattan Institute, 213
Osborn, John Jay, Jr. (b. 1945), writer, 78
Otway, Thomas (1652–1685), English dramatist, 160
Ouida (1839–1908), Scottish writer, 261
Ovid (43 B.C.–17 A.D.), Roman poet, 32
Packard, Edward B. Jr., American lawyer, 138
Paine, Thomas (1737–1819), British-born American political philosopher and writer, 130
Palmer, Harry (b. 1939), American lawyer, 58
Pankhurst, Emmeline (1858–1928), English suffragist, 158
Papantonio, Mike (b. 1953), American lawyer, 216
Pavalon, Eugene (b. 1933), American lawyer and President, American Trial Lawyer's Association, 196
Perry, Robert, American lawyer, 109
Phillips, Wendell (1811–1884), American orator and reformer, 145

Plato (427–347 B.C.), 1st-century Greek Philosopher, 17
Pollock, Frederick (1845–1937), English judge, 185
Polsby, Daniel, law professor, Northwestern Univ., 104
Pomerantz, Hart, American lawyer, 137
Pound, Roscoe (1870–1964), Dean Emeritus, Harvard Law School, 26, 261
Powell, Adam Clayton, Jr. (1908–1972), American clergyman and United States Congressman, 148
Powell, Lewis F., Jr. (b. 1907), Supreme Court Justice, 114, 116
Powell, Thomas Reed (1880–1955), professor, Harvard University, 49
Prosser, William L., legal scholar, 52
Quayle, J. Danforth (b. 1947), 44th Vice President of the United States, 186, 242
Quinn, Jane Bryant (b. 1939), American journalist, 38, 244
Reagan, Ronald W. (b. 1911), 40th President of the United States, 259
Rehnquist, William H. (b. 1924), Supreme Court Justice, 83, 258
Ricker, Darlene (b. 1954), American lawyer and legal journalist, 83, 230
Rinehart, Mary Roberts (1876–1958), American writer, 44
Robbins, Tom (b. 1936), American writer, 67
Rochefoucauld, François de la (1613–1680), French writer, 163
Rockefeller, John D., Jr. (1874–1960), American oil magnate and philanthropist, 130
Rodell, Fred (1907–1980), law professor, Yale University, 18, 213
Rogers, Will (1879–1935), American actor and humorist, 53, 68, 126, 216
Roland, Jeanne-Marie (1754–1793), French revolutionary, 176
Roosevelt, Theodore (1858–1919), 26th President of the United States, 30, 147
Root, Elihu (1845–1937), American lawyer and statesman, 66
Rosten, Leo (b. 1908), Polish-American writer, 69
Rothman, David, American lawyer, 252
Rousseau, Jean Jacques (1712–1778), French philosopher and writer, 20
Rubin, Asher (b. 1936), California Deputy Attorney General, 186
Rubin, Ellis (b. 1925), American lawyer, 38
Rymer, Pamela Ann (b. 1941), Los Angeles Federal judge, 122, 211
Sandburg, Carl (1878–1967), American writer, 47
Sanger, Margaret (1883–1966), American political activist, 245

Sawyer, Diane (b. 1945), American television journalist, 224
Scalia, Antonin (b. 1936), Supreme Court Justice, 25
Scarman, Lord Leslie (b. 1911), English lawyer, 258
Schulder, Diane B. (b. 1937), American lawyer and educator, 245
Schwartz, Michael Alan (b. 1948), American journalist, 125
Scott, Sir Walter (1771–1832), Scottish poet and writer, 56
Seebach, Linda, American journalist, 186
Seneca (4 B.C.–65 A.D.), Roman statesman and philosopher, 85, 175
Shapiro, Irving S. (b. 1916), American industrialist, 187
Shapiro, Robert (b. 1942), Defense Lawyer in the O.J Simpson Trial, 233
Shays, Ruth, 241, 258
Shea, Edward F., Jr. (b. 1925), American lawyer, 210
Sherman, Charles E., American lawyer, 234
Sherman, Norm, American lawyer, 139
Singer, Alyson, American lawyer, 25
Smiles, Samuel (1812–1904), English writer, 33
Smith, Elliott Dunlap (1891–1976), American writer, 214
Smith, Sydney (1771–1845), English writer, 32, 257
Socrates, 4th-Century B.C, Greek philosopher, 167
Solzhenitsyn, Alexander (b. 1918), Russian writer, 238, 252
Sophocles (496–406 B.C.), Greek dramatist, 121
Soucy, Dave (b. 1955), American lawyer, 55
Spence, Gerry (b. 1929), American lawyer, 138, 230, 232
Spencer, Herbert (1820–1903), English philosopher, 103
Spicer, David (b. 1948), American lawyer, 161
Stanton, Elizabeth Cady (1815–1902), American suffragist, 145
Starr, Kenneth, (b. 1946), Special Prosecutor, 149
Stein, Sol, American businessman and writer, 47
Steinem, Gloria (b. 1934), American writer and feminist, 259
Stempel, Jeff, Florida State University, Law Professor, 225
Sterling, John (1844–1918), American lawyer, 67
Stevenson, Adlai E. (1900–1965), American lawyer and diplomat, 78, 109, 214

Stevenson, Melford (b. 1902), British judge, 195
Stewart, E. Ralph, 239
Stewart, Potter (1915–1985), Supreme Court Justice, 92, 159
Stratcher, Cameron, American lawyer, 188
Stryker, Lloyd Paul (b. 1955), American lawyer, 195
Solzhenitsyn, Aleksandr I., Russian writer
Surtees, Robert Smith (1806–1864), 19th-century English novelist, 53
Sykes, Charles, American author, 73
Syrus, Publilius, 1st-century B.C. Roman writer, 87, 89, 150
Szasz, Thomas, professor, Syracuse University, 150
Tacitus (c. 56–120), Roman historian, 88
Taft, William Howard (1857–1930), 27th President of the United States, 192
Theognis, 6th-century B.C. Greek poet, 160
Thomas, H. James (b. 1960), American lawyer, 58
Thompson, James R. (b. 1936), Illinois Governor, 252
Thoreau, Henry David (1817–1862), American writer, 27, 177
Tocqueville, Alexis de (1805–1859), French statesman and writer, 102, 248
Tolstoy, Leo (1828–1910), 19th-century Russian philosopher and author, 134
Townsend, Robert (b. 1920), American businessman, 45
Train, Arthur (1875–1945), lawyer and writer, 54
Traver, Robert (1903–1993), American writer and judge, 79
Trillin, Calvin, American writer, 140
Trollope, Anthony (1815–1882), English writer, 225
Truman, Harry S (1884–1972), 33rd President of the United States, 117
Turow, Scott (b. 1949), American lawyer and writer, 39
Twain, Mark (1835–1910), American writer and humorist, 45, 101, 249
Tweed, Harrison (1885–1969), American lawyer, 45
Udall, Morris K. (b. 1922), United States Congressman, 116
Veeck, Bill (1914–1986), owner, Chicago White Sox, 242
Vidal, Gore (b. 1925), American writer, 187
Voltaire (1694–1778), French writer, 31, 189, 243
Wapner, Joseph A. (b. 1919), American judge, 84, 210, 239

Warren, Earl (1891–1974), Supreme Court Justice, 123
Wartowski, Thomas, American lawyer, 17, 100
Washington, George (1732–1799), 1st President of the United States, 149, 168
Waters, John (b. 1946), American filmmaker, 195
Webster, Daniel (1782–1852), American statesman, orator, and lawyer, 20, 39, 122, 230, 269
Weinberger, Caspar W. (b. 1917), publisher, 187
Weinkrantz, Herman, American judge, 158
Wells, Ida B. (1862–1931), American journalist, 175
Whalen, Grover A. (1886–1962), New York City police commissioner, 144
Whichcote, Benjamin (1609–1683), English philosophical theologian, 90
White, Daniel R. (b. 1953), American writer, 138
Whitman, Walt (1819–1892), American poet, 159
Wilde, Oscar (1854–1900), Irish writer, 234
Wills, Garry, Northwestern University history professor, 135
Wilson, Frank W. (b. 1917), American judge, 164
Wilson, Woodrow (1856–1924), 28th President of the United States, 159, 231
Wycherley, William (1640–1716), English dramatist, 55
Wydick, Richard, American lawyer, 72
Yevtushenko, Yevgeny (b. 1933), Russian poet, 160
Younger, Evelle J., American lawyer, 245
Yutang, Lin, Chinese writer, 168
Yuter, S. C., American journalist and writer, 26
Zagrans, Eric (b. 1953), American lawyer, 110
Zerman, Melvyn B. (b. 1930), American writer, 103
Zobel, Hiller B. (b. 1932), American judge, 202
Zuckerman, Mortimer (b. 1937), American journalist, 17

ABOUT THE AUTHORS

Bruce Nash and **Allan Zullo** have co-authored more than sixty books together, including the best-selling *Sports Hall of Shame* and *Amazing But True* series. Bruce lives in Los Angeles where he produces and writes television programs.

Allan writes both adult and children's books and lives near Asheville, North Carolina, with his wife, collaborator **Kathryn Zullo**, an editorial researcher.